Sharing Circles:

Guided Discussions for Teaching Emotional Intelligence

Susanna Palomares & David Cowan

INNERCHOICE Publishing

Cover Design – Linda Thille

ISBN – 10: 1-56499-061-7
ISBN – 13: 978-1-56499-061-7

INNERCHOICE Publishing
15079 Oak Chase Court
Wellington, FL 33414

www.InnerchoicePublishing.com

PUBLISHING.

. . . given the crises we find
ourselves and our children facing,
and given the quantum of hope held out by
courses in emotional literacy,
we must ask ourselves:
Shouldn't we be teaching
these most essential skills
for life to every child—
now more than ever?

And if not now, when?

Daniel Goleman

Contents

Sharing Circle Topics

An Introduction to Emotional Intelligence

Intelligence is more than we thought it was. As we look at intelligence today, it's clear that it really is not just one dimensional. Traditionally when we talk about intelligence or indicate that a person is intelligent, what do we say? How do we describe an intelligent person? What characteristics do these people have? Invariably, as these questions are answered, we find ourselves using comparative terms, and, more likely than not, we find ourselves, at some point, referring to the measurement of intelligence we know as IQ. But there is more.

We already know from our own experiences in the world that it takes more than just being smart or having a high IQ to be successful. As we have all seen, some of our brightest students have failed to experience the success in life that we would have predicted for them using traditional measurements. Research now tells us that, at most, IQ contributes to only about 20 percent to the factors that determine success — leaving 80 percent to other forces. These forces make up what is called emotional intelligence. Many schools are adding emotional intelligence to their definition of what it means to be smart.

What then is emotional intelligence and how can it be developed?

To answer this question we must start by looking at how important our emotions, and feelings, are in determining our behavior.

Recognizing the Importance of Emotions and Feelings

Try this little exercise. On a blank sheet of paper draw a line down the center. Label the left side Feelings, and the right side Actions. On the left side, write a list of as many of the feelings you can remember that you've had today. Leave a few spaces between the words. You may think of a feeling you had in traffic getting to school, or a response to a student, etc. Take only a minute to write this list of feeling words.

Now move to the action side. Pick out one positive feeling you wrote, and opposite it in the action column, write what you remember you did in response to that feeling. You may have laughed, said thanks, etc.

Next, pick one feeling that was not pleasant and write down what you did.

Now, pick out the feeling that made you most uncomfortable and write down what you did.

Can you see how absolutely our actions are connected to our feelings? We all respond to our feelings, not in the exact same way, but we all do respond. Our feelings flow from our emotions. All people have the same emotions. Things like love, hate, fear, etc. The feelings people have as they experience these emotions can vary as can their behaviors in response to these feelings. Emotions generate our feelings, and our feelings are messages that tell us that we are experiencing an emotional event. *It is what we do in response to these feeling messages that is a measure of our emotional intelligence.*

Importance of Feelings to Children

Think for a minute how this idea applies to children.

When psychologist Walter Mischel started an experiment with preschoolers at Stanford University, he was interested in observing how four year olds handled their impulses. Individual children were told that they could have two marshmallows if they would wait for the experimenter to run an errand. If they couldn't wait, they could have one marshmallow, but they could have it right then. The children were each given one marshmallow and told that if they waited until the errand was run to eat it, they could have a second one. Imagine the temptation, the struggle between immediate and delayed gratification even with the reward of an additional treat.

Some of the children (about a third) ate the marshmallow right away. Others — determined to wait — covered their eyes, put their heads down, sang to themselves, tried to sleep, and walked around the room. Science then waited for these students to grow up.

Fourteen years later when the students were in high-school, a survey of parents and teachers found some remarkable differences between the two groups. Those children who held out for the second marshmallow generally grew up to be better adjusted, more popular, adventurous, confident and dependable teenagers. The children who gave in to temptation early were more likely to be lonely, easily frustrated, and stubborn. They struggled under stress and rejected challenges. On the SAT, the kids who held out scored an average of 210 points higher. At age four, this simple experiment proved to be twice as accurate a predictor of performance on SAT's than did IQ. It was only after children learned to read that IQ became an accurate predictor of performance. This suggests that managing one's responses to the feelings of impulse by delaying gratification casts a long shadow over an individual's ability to perform. In quoting Walter Mischel, Daniel Goleman in his book Emotional Intelligence states, "'Goal-directed self-imposed delay of gratification' is perhaps the essence of emotional self-regulation: the ability to deny impulse in the service of a goal, whether it be building a business, solving an algebraic equation, or pursuing the Stanley Cup." Mischel's findings underscore the role of emotional intelligence as a meta-ability, determining how well or how poorly people are able to use their other mental capacities.

It seems the ability to delay gratification is a master skill. It is the success of the reasoning part of the brain over the emotional part. It is a sign of emotional intelligence. It does not show up on an IQ test.

Think for a minute about the implications of this to what children need to learn — to what we need to teach. What a gift we give to children when we help them learn to channel their feelings into positive behaviors and develop self-control.

The Emotional Mind

IQ: Most of us use this term. What does it mean? In the simplest terms it is a measurement of the capacity to acquire and apply knowledge; the faculty of thought and reason. It is the ratio of a child's tested mental age to his or her chronological age. What then is EQ?

EQ is another way of being smart. It is the capacity to know and manage one's emotions, to marshal emotions in the service of goals. It's empathy and being able to recognize emotions in others and to effectively handle relationships.

These two types of intelligence must work together. IQ has more to do with the rational, reasoning mind while EQ has more to do with the emotional mind. Evidence now demonstrates that the emotional mind has the power to override rational intelligence for both good and bad consequences. It is this power that amplifies the importance of developing emotional intelligence.

The emotional brain has two interdependent parts that come together in what is known as the reticular function. The first part with the amygdala playing a key role, acts like a sentry, warning of danger. The second part with the neocortex as the central player, functions like a strategist, deciding on courses of action. It is important to note that action taken can be unconscious as in reactions and impulse behavior, or it can be conscious; the product of thoughtful and considered choice. Together, the sentry and strategist govern our behavior for good or ill.

Strategist: Decides on the course of action.

Sentry: Warns of danger.

The Impact of Emotional Intelligence

Because of their connection to behavior, emotions impact every area of life: health, learning, achievement, and relationships.

Managing feelings well and recognizing and responding effectively to the feelings of others enables children to lead happy and productive lives and to master habits of mind that contribute to personal and career success. We all, parents and educators, must nurture emotional intelligence in the same caring way we nurture IQ.

Most people are simply unaware of the implications and impact of emotions on health, learning, behavior and relationships. The research is rich with examples, but the end result is that people with more highly developed emotional competence have better health, do better at learning, exhibit behavior that is contributing and pro-social, and are able to establish more meaningful, longer lasting relationships. With all this standing in its favor the development of EQ is as important as the consideration of IQ particularly when its contribution to academic performance and intellectual growth are so vital.

Emotional Intelligence is Learned

The part of the brain responsible for emotional response is among the last to become anatomically mature and continues to develop into adolescence. It is evident that when emotional lessons are repeated in a child's life the brain develops circuitry that wires in a specific response.

A child may learn that if you're angry you yell or hit, or if you're frustrated, you give up. Without intervention these will become his or her response habits throughout life. However, if a child can learn positive ways to handle anger, frustration and other emotions, these skills will serve this person well in any life endeavor, relationship or any other experience. Learning positive, pro-social responses is not generally done on one's own. These skills are learned through interaction with other children and adults. This is why it's critical that we help children learn all the skills of emotional intelligence. And the sooner we begin to teach appropriate responses, the sooner and easier they will become part of children's internal response systems.

All this is not to suggest that once an individual reaches adulthood that the neural circuitry and, therefore, learned response can't be reshaped. It is a fact, however, that as we grow older, the ability to relearn, reshape and even acquire emotional intelligence becomes more difficult. This is another reason why it is so important that we begin a purposeful and systematic effort to provide opportunity for emotional learning in early childhood, and in elementary school and continues through middle- and high-schools.

Working with Emotions

The primary goal of emotional education is to improve the skills of the strategist — the neocortex. As the neocortex becomes increasingly able to manage the sentry — the fast-trigger amygdala — students learn to manage their behaviors more appropriately. Studies have proven that when students are able to rein in impulses and otherwise manage negative behavior, their academic achievement scores and school performance improve.

As educators, it is easy to think of examples of out-of-control emotions you see acted out in your schools.

Using the theory of emotional intelligence, we can make a difference in the lives of students. There are three primary areas in which we can have tremendous impact. We know that emotional competence begins with greater self awareness. This is followed by developing the ability to understand and manage emotions and to control impulses. Last, is the building of relationship skills. These are the areas that we can work on in school which will help students develop emotional competence that will serve them throughout their entire lives.

Self Awareness:

How do we help children gain self awareness? Try this. Imagine you are a long green caterpillar and that you are crawling along a tree branch. All of a sudden you see a bird land on a branch near you. What are you feeling right now?

Surely, you can describe the feelings you have. That is what children need to be able to do. They need a vocabulary of words that describe emotions. Words are the only tool we have for systematically turning our attention and awareness to the feelings within us, and for describing and reflecting on our thoughts and behaviors. When we inwardly sense an idea we can't put into words, we struggle to find the words. Without words, we can't deal with the idea, share it with others, or clarify its meaning for ourselves. The effective use of words constitutes the first step in developing the ability to grasp previously unspoken feelings and understand the connection between feelings and behavior.

For students to be able to manage their feelings, they must know what those feelings are. To know what they are, they must practice describing them in words. When a particular feeling is grasped in words several times, the mind soon begins to automatically recall ideas and concepts in association with the feeling and can start to provide ways of dealing with the feeling; e.g., "I'm feeling angry and I need to get away from this situation to calm down."

With practice, the mind becomes more and more adept at making these connections. When a recognized feeling comes up, the mind can sort through alternative responses to the feeling. As a student practices this response sequence in reaction to a variety of feelings, he will find words floating into consciousness that accurately identify what is going on emotionally and physically for him. This knowledge in turn develops the capacity to think before and during action. The ability to put words to feelings, to understand those words, to sort through an internal repertoire of responses and to choose appropriate, responsible behavior in reaction to a feeling indicates a high level of emotional intelligence.

One of the main objectives of the Sharing Circles in this book is to provide a consistent, structured and safe place for students to develop self awareness and a feeling vocabulary through sharing their feelings, thoughts and experiences (and listening to others do the same).

Self Management:

Self management has to do with learning to manage our responses to the feeling messages our emotions give to us. Not all emotions require the same kind or degree of control. Those we want to focus on are the ones that get in the way of or compromise our abilities to perform. Whether children, teens, or adults, managing distressing moods well and controlling impulses is of critical importance. Why don't we begin by looking at two related emotions that are actually at opposite ends of the emotional scale. One is anger, the other is sadness.

Let's focus on managing anger first. Anger is at the high-arousal end of the emotional spectrum.

Try this. Think of yourself driving down a busy road and you notice in your rearview mirror another driver who is following you way too closely. This driver continues to "ride your bumper" and then suddenly passes you and cuts you off. Take a moment right now and think about your first feeling and impulse for action. Be honest.

Would you act on this first impulse or feeling? If you don't, then you'll need to do something else. What is it? What do you do?

In the past, we thought teaching strategies to use in situations like these was enough, but we've come to understand two things. First, the emotional content of some situations allows our *sentry* (the amygdala) to overwhelm our neocortex *strategist*. In these cases we don't do what we know is best, we do whatever it is we've learned to react with, our response habits. This means that it is not enough just to know what to do. In fact, research indicates that very often people who do regrettable things in response to highly emotional situations actually know better ways of responding but fail to use them. Acting out is often something children do as they *react* in response to things going on in their lives. Rather than *act*, using the thoughtfulness of the *strategist*, behavior is orchestrated by the unconscious influence of the *sentry*.

This leads us to the second understanding. That is, that we must teach students a single method for establishing emotional control first before they can then focus on appropriate responses. We need to know how we can teach students to successfully get a hold on their impulses to act. The topics provided in this book allow students the opportunity to first understand that feelings are messages that can help them maintain control of emotional situations thus permitting the

strategist to shape appropriate responses to emotional situations and suppress the *sentry's* efforts to take control. Second, students begin to develop the master skill of *buying time* that lets them take the time necessary to act rather than react in these situations. This single approach becomes the gateway skill, and the key to self management and control.

The other emotion is sadness which is a state of low arousal that depresses the minds ability to deal effectively in almost all areas. It can produce lethargy, reduce the ability to reason and respond, and it can lead to despondency or even depression.

The first key to responding to impulsive behavior associated with highly emotional events or to the depressed state brought on by sadness is to be aware that we are experiencing them. We learn to be aware through discussing our feelings and listening as others discuss their feelings. Students experiencing anger need to have internal skills and an external support system to process feelings and to avoid accumulation of anger. Letting it all out is not helpful. They must learn the master strategy of buying some time. Time to let the chemistry of either anger or sadness dissipate. They need to learn to re-frame situations so that they can be seen from a positive perspective.

In this book our aim is to accomplish both skill development and the means to control the *sentry* so that the *strategist* can help children respond appropriately in challenging situations. By participating in Sharing Circles, students have many opportunities to focus on their feelings, thoughts, and behaviors, and those of others. Through regular verbal sharing, they develop an awareness of their feelings, they talk about their responses, and they listen to how others have responded in similar situations. Their repertoire of feeling words increases as does their ability to differentiate between appropriate and inappropriate behaviors and, thus, learn *awarenesses* and *strategies* that help them manage emotions and control impulses.

Relationship Skills:

The last area we must attend to in helping students develop emotional competencies is a big one called relationship skills. It includes such skills as empathy, influence, cooperation, conflict resolution, and listening.

Relating effectively to others is a challenge we all face. People who are effective in their social interactions have the ability to understand others. They know how to be cooperative with others and interact flexibly, skillfully, and responsibly. At the same time, they recognize their own needs and maintain their own integrity. Socially effective people can process the nonverbal as well as verbal messages of others. They possess the very important awareness

that all people have the power to affect one another. They are aware of not only how others affect them, but the effects their behaviors have on others which is vital in conflict resolution.

The Sharing Circle process has been designed so that healthy, responsible behaviors are modeled by the teacher or counselor in his or her role as leader. The rules also require that the students relate positively and effectively to one another. This process brings out and affirms the positive qualities inherent in everyone and allows students to practice effective modes of communication. Because Sharing Circles provide a place where participants are listened to and their feelings accepted, students learn how to provide the same conditions to peers and adults outside the group.

One of the great benefits of the Sharing Circle process is that it does not merely teach young people about social interaction, it lets them interact! Every circle is a real-life experience of social interaction where the students share, listen, explore, plan, dream, and problem solve together. As they interact, they learn about each other and they realize what it takes to relate effectively to others. Any given discussion may provide a dozen tiny flashes of positive interpersonal insight for an individual participant. Gradually, the reality of what constitutes effective behavior in relating to others is internalized.

Through this regular sharing of interpersonal experiences, the students learn that behavior can be positive or negative, and sometimes both at the same time. Consequences can be constructive, destructive, or both. Different people respond differently to the same event. They have different feelings and thoughts. The students begin to understand what will cause what to happen; they grasp the concept of cause and effect; they see themselves affecting others and being affected by others.

The ability to make accurate interpretations and responses in social interactions allows students to know where they stand with themselves and with others. They can tell what actions "fit" a situation. Sharing Circles are marvelous testing grounds where students can observe themselves and others in action, and can begin to see themselves as contributing to the good and bad feelings of others. Sharing Circles can also noticeably accelerate the development and internalization of conflict resolution skills and strategies. With this understanding, students are helped to conclude that being responsible towards others feels good, and is the most valuable and personally rewarding form of interaction.

Listening:

This is one of the most important skills students need to develop. It transcends and affects all the skills and attributes of emotional intelligence. Unfortunately many individuals develop poor listening habits early on that shape their listening skills for the rest of their lives. As a component of one's emotional intellect, listening adds value in two critical areas. First, it is the primary skill necessary for developing and maintaining interpersonal relationships. It is through good listening that we express caring, that we let others know how much we value them and the things they share with us, it is the most important element in establishing trust with others, and it lets those we listen to know that we are willing to give time, our most important possession, to attending to what they have to say. This and our nonverbal abilities add far more to the value of our communication and relationships than words alone.

Second, skillful listening is a principal means of learning. It is required to gain emotional and cognitive competencies, and its absence impedes learning and destroys communication.

Sadly, listening skills, though often acknowledged, are seldom taught. Because of the strategies employed in this book, listening skills are either principal objectives or secondary outcomes of every Sharing Circle in which students engage. Listening skills develop only through good modelling and continued practice, and as with language, these skills are more easily learned when young that at any other time in life. Just as these Sharing Circles provide a process for students to learn about themselves through self-expression and exploration, it also teaches students how to be good listeners. The rules of listening to the person who is speaking, without probing, put-downs, or interruptions demand that each student give active attention to the speaker. Through the regular practice of good listening skills and the positive modeling of active listening by the teacher or counselor leading the circle, the students begin to internalize good listening habits.

The key to all of this is adherence to the rules and, of course, regular participation in the Sharing Circle process. Skills and knowledge are developed over time through regular, sustained participation. These benefits are the same for all ages from elementary through high-school and beyond.

Educating the Emotional Mind

It is difficult if not impossible to have new curriculum content added to an already full teaching or counseling schedule. However, since feelings are a part of everything we do, they can be a part of everything we teach and learn.

Now that we know that they are important and necessary to ensure success for students, we can incorporate the three broad areas of emotional intelligence (Developing self awareness, learning to manage emotions and control impulses, and building relationship skills) into traditional subject areas.

Incorporating emotional content into the curriculum can close the gap between academic knowledge and life experience. It can make curriculum come alive and give students a clearer picture concerning how they will apply academic knowledge.

How do we do this? We can do it by asking students to identify their own feelings and to speculate about the feelings of others — adults, classmates, story characters, contemporary and historical figures, etc. — relating feelings to actions and actions to consequences. We can challenge students to evaluate realistic alternatives and speculate as to their effects. We can talk about things we observe as we watch students in action, surfacing issues for discussion. These strategies can be used with any subject area.

The activities you'll find in this book use Sharing Circles as the learning strategy. As students use their own frames of reference, they will be able to make impactful connections between the concepts presented and the roles that they have played and will continue to play in shaping their life experiences. These Sharing Circles provide powerful learning experiences while promoting a broad range of skill development and practice. Each circle also engages students in the development of critical or higher order thinking skills as they engage in extracting insights and drawing conclusions regarding the topics of discussion.

Benefits

One of the most important outcomes in schools where emotional competency is taught is a drop in the fighting and suspension rates. As they acquire emotional competencies, individual students demonstrate gains in academic performance. Personal benefits accrue also. Students are more skilled at making friends and are better family members. In addition, they develop into more desirable workers, mates, bosses and citizens.

Here are some of the advantages identified in each of these areas. They are the summary of evaluation results:

Emotional Self Awareness
- Improvement in recognizing and naming own emotions
- Better able to understand the causes of feelings
- Recognizing the difference between feelings and action

Managing Emotions
- Better frustration tolerance and anger management
- Fewer verbal put-downs, fights, and classroom disruptions
- Better able to express anger appropriately, without fighting
- Fewer suspensions and expulsions
- Less aggressive or self-destructive behavior
- More positive feelings about self, school, and family
- Better at handling stress
- Less loneliness and social anxiety

Harnessing Emotions Productively
- More responsible
- Better able to focus on the task at hand and pay attention
- Less impulsive, more self-control
- Improved scores on achievement

Empathy: Reading Emotions
- Better able to take another person's perspective
- Improved empathy and sensitivity to others' feelings
- Better at listening to others

Handling Relationships
- Increased ability to analyze and understand relationships
- Better at resolving conflicts and negotiating disagreements
- Better at solving problems in relationships
- More assertive and skilled at communicating
- More popular and outgoing; friendly and involved with peers
- More sought out by peers
- More concerned and considerate
- More pro-social and harmonious in groups
- More sharing, cooperation, and helpfulness
- More democratic

These conclusions have been compiled from objective evaluations comparing experimental and control groups and by measuring the behavior of students before and after receiving instruction geared to developing emotional competencies.

With these kinds of outcomes at stake the argument for helping students acquire broad emotional competencies and higher levels of emotional intelligence are compelling. The material you have here will produce for you and for your students these kinds of results if it is integrated into the rigors of teaching and learning. The value more than offsets the effort. The rewards far outshine the cost. These are the skills and attributes that transcend all other learning and permit your students to achieve at higher levels academically and socially than ever before.

Sharing Circles:
The EQ Super Strategy

Sharing Circles as presented in this book are a unique small-group discussion process in which participants (including the leader) share their thoughts, feelings, experiences, and insights in response to specific, assigned topics. Sharing Circles are loosely structured, and participants are expected to adhere to rules that promote the goals of positive interaction while specifically assuring cooperation, effective communication, trust, and confidentiality.

The nature of the Sharing Circle— the messages it sends to students and the behaviors it encourages and discourages are highly conducive to social-emotional growth. Students follow clear rules of conduct, accept ownership of those rules, are supportive of one another, and experience a sense of satisfaction by complying with the guidelines and procedures. Regular participation in Sharing Circles can noticeably accelerate the development and internalization of the qualities and skills of emotional intelligence.

Two Initial Pointers

To prepare yourself to take full advantage of these discussions, thoroughly read and digest the section entitled How to Lead a Sharing Circle which begins on page 19. As you are reading, keep two points in mind:

First, the topic elaborations provided under the heading, "Introducing the Topic," are guides for you to follow when presenting the topic to your students. They are excellent models, but need not be read verbatim. The idea is to focus the attention and thoughts of students on the specific topic to be discussed. *In your elaboration, use language and examples that are appropriate to the age, ability, and culture of your students.*

Second, we strongly urge you to respect the integrity of the sharing and discussion phases of the process. These two phases are procedurally and qualitatively different, yet of equal importance in promoting awareness, insight, and higher-level thinking in students. After you have led several circles, you will appreciate the instructional advantage of maintaining this unique relationship.

All topics are intended to develop awareness and insight through voluntary sharing. This occurs in the first (or sharing) phase of the Sharing Circle. The discussion question phase, for which specific questions are provided, allows students to understand what has been shared at deeper levels, to evaluate ideas that have been generated by the topic, and to apply specific concepts to other areas of learning.

Key Outcomes

As students follow the rules and relate to each other verbally during the Sharing Circle, they are practicing respectful listening and oral communication. As they listen carefully while other students ponder and discuss the various topics, the students have repeated opportunities to mentally take the perspective of others. They are also required to demonstrate awareness and control over their own feelings, thoughts, and behaviors during the discussion. Through the positive experience of give and take, they learn the importance of interacting responsibly and effectively.

The topics offered in this book address many qualities inherent in people with well developed emotional intelligence— keeping agreements, developing responsible habits, solving problems, demonstrating respect for self and others, being loyal, being trustworthy and honest, following rules, demonstrating kindness and consideration, resolving conflicts, etc.

As students learn to relate effectively to others, issues related to acceptable and unacceptable behavior surface again and again. Students learn that all people have the power to influence one another. They become aware not only of how others affect them, but of the effects their behaviors have on others.

The Sharing Circle process has been designed so that healthy, responsible behaviors are modeled by the teacher or counselor in his or her role as leader. Also, the rules require that the students relate responsibly and effectively to one another. The process brings out and affirms the positive qualities inherent in everyone and allows students to practice effective modes of communication. Because Sharing Circles provide a place where participants are listened to and their feelings accepted, students learn how to provide the same conditions to peers and adults in interactions beyond the Sharing Circle sessions.

Sharing Circles teach cooperation and promote caring. As equitably as possible, the structure attempts to meet the needs of all participants. Everyone's feelings are accepted; everyone's contributions are judged valuable. The Sharing Circle group is not another competitive arena, but is guided by a spirit of collaboration. When students practice fair, respectful interaction with one another, they benefit from the experience and are likely to employ these responsible behaviors in other life situations.

What You Need to Know About Sharing Circles

Group Size and Composition

This is a time for focusing on individuals' contributions in an unhurried fashion. For this reason, each Sharing Circle session needs to be kept relatively small—eight to twelve usually works best. Once they move beyond the primary grades, students are capable of extensive verbalization. You will want to encourage this, and not stifle them because of time constraints.

Each group should be as heterogeneous as possible with respect to sex, ability, and racial/ethnic background. Sometimes there will be a group in which all the students are particularly reticent to speak. At these times, bring in an expressive student or two who will get things going. Sometimes it is necessary for practical reasons to change the membership of a group. Once established, however, it is advisable to keep a group as stable as possible.

Length and Location

Most sessions last approximately 10 to 20 minutes. At first students tend to be reluctant to express themselves fully because they do not yet know that this is a safe place. Consequently your first sessions may not last more than 10 minutes. Generally speaking, students become comfortable and motivated to speak with continued experience.

In middle- and high-school classrooms, Sharing Circles may be conducted at any time during the class period. Starting circle sessions at the beginning of the period allows additional time in case students become deeply involved in the topic. If you start late in the period, make sure the students are aware of their responsibility to be concise.

In elementary classes, any time of day is appropriate for Sharing Circles. Some teachers like to set the tone for the day by beginning with this process; others feel it's a perfect way to complete the day and to send the students away with positive feelings.

Sharing Circles may be carried out wherever there is room for students to sit in a circle and experience few or no distractions. Most leaders prefer to have students sit in chairs rather than on the floor. Students seem to be less apt to invade one another's space while seated in chairs. Some leaders conduct sessions outdoors, with students seated in a secluded, grassy area.

How to Involve All the Students

Teachers and counselors have used numerous methods to involve students in Sharing Circles. What works well for one leader or class does not always work for another. Here are two basic strategies leaders have successfully used to get groups started. Whichever you use, we recommend that you post a chart listing the rules and procedures to which every participant may refer.

1. Divide the class into groups of 8 to 12 students. Start one group at a time and cycle through all groups. If possible, provide an opportunity for every student to experience a Sharing Circle in a setting where there are no disturbances. This may mean arranging for another staff member or aide to take charge of the students not participating in the Sharing Circle. Non-participants may work on course work or silent reading, or if you have a cooperative librarian,

they may be sent to the library to work independently or in small groups on a class assignment. Repeat this procedure until all of the students have been involved in at least one circle session.

Next, initiate a class discussion about the process. Explain that from now on you will be meeting with each Sharing Circle group in the classroom, with the remainder of the class present. Ask the students to help you plan established procedures for the remainder of the class to follow.

Meet with each Sharing Circle group on a different day, systematically cycling through the groups.

2. Combine an inner discussion group with an outer circle. Conduct a Sharing Circle with the inner group while those in the outer group listen and observe. Then have the two groups change places, with the students on the outside becoming the inner discussion group, and responding verbally to the topic. If you run out of time in middle- or high-school classrooms, use two class periods for this. Later, a third group may be added to this alternating cycle. The end product of this arrangement is two or more groups (comprising everyone in the class) meeting together simultaneously. While one group is involved in discussion, the other groups listen and observe as members of an outer group.

What To Do With the Rest of the Class

A number of arrangements can be made for students who are not participating in Sharing Circles. Here are some ideas:

- Arrange the room to ensure privacy. This may involve placing a circle of chairs or carpeting in a corner, away from other work areas. You might construct dividers from existing furniture, such as bookshelves or screens, or simply arrange chairs and tables in such a way that the Sharing Circle discussion area is protected from distractions.

- Involve aides, counselors, parents, or fellow teachers. Have an aide conduct a lesson with the rest of the class while you meet with a Sharing Circle group. If you do not have an aide assigned to you, use auxiliary staff or parent volunteers.

- Have students work quietly on subject-area assignments in pairs or small, task-oriented groups.

- Utilize student aides or leaders. If the seat-work activity is in a content area, appoint students who show ability in that area as "consultants," and have them assist other students.

- Give the students plenty to do. List academic activities on the board. Make materials for quiet individual activities available so that students cannot run out of things to do and be tempted to consult you or disturb others.

- Make the activity of students outside the Sharing Circle group enjoyable. When you can involve the rest of the class in something meaningful to them, students will probably be less likely to interrupt the discussion.

- Have the students work on an ongoing project. When they have a task in progress, students can simply resume where they left off, with little or no introduction from you. In these cases, appointing a "person in charge," "group leader," or "consultant" is wise.

- Allow individual journal-writing. While a Sharing Circle is in progress, have the other students make entries in a private (or share-with-teacher-only) journal. The topic for journal writing could be the same topic that is being discussed in the Sharing Circle. Do not correct the journals, but if you read them, be sure to respond to the entries with your own written thoughts, where appropriate.

How to Lead a Sharing Circle

This section is a thorough guide for conducting Sharing Circles. It covers major points to keep in mind and answers questions which will arise as you begin using the program. Please remember that these guidelines are presented to assist you, not to restrict you. Follow them, and trust your own leadership style at the same time.

The Sharing Circle is a structured communication process that provides students a safe place for learning about life and developing important aspects of social-emotional learning.

First, we'll provide a brief overview of the process of leading a Sharing Circle and then we'll cover each step in more detail.

A Sharing Circle begins when a group of students and the adult leader sit down together in a circle so that each person is able to see the others easily. The leader of the Sharing Circle briefly greets and welcomes each individual, conveying a feeling of enthusiasm blended with seriousness.

When everyone appears comfortable, the leader takes a few moments to review the Sharing Circle Rules. These rules inform the students of the positive behaviors required of them and guarantees the emotional safety and security, and equality of each member.

After the students understand and agree to follow the rules, the leader announces the topic for the session. A brief elaboration of the topic follows in which the leader provides examples and possibly mentions the topics relationship to prior topics or to other things the students are involved in. Then the leader re-states the topic and allows a little silence during which circle members may review and ponder their own related memories and mentally prepare their verbal response to the topic. (The topics and elaborations are provided in this curriculum.)

Next, the leader invites the circle participants to voluntarily share their responses to the topic, one at a time. No one is forced to share, but everyone is given an opportunity to share while all the other circle members listen attentively. The circle participants tell the group about themselves, their personal experiences, thoughts, feelings, hopes and dreams as they relate to the topic. Most of the circle time is devoted to this sharing phase because of its central importance.

During this time, the leader assumes a dual role—that of leader and participant. The leader makes sure that everyone who wishes to speak is given the opportunity while simultaneously enforcing the rules as necessary. The leader also takes a turn to speak if he or she wishes.

After everyone who wants to share has done so, the leader introduces the next phase of the Sharing Circle by asking several discussion questions. This phase represents a transition to the intellectual mode and allows participants to reflect on and express learnings gained from the sharing phase and encourages participants to combine cognitive abilities and emotional experiencing. It's in this phase that participants are able to crystallize learnings and to understand the relevance of the discussion to their daily lives. (Discussion questions for each topic are provided in this curriculum.)

When the students have finished discussing their responses to the questions and the session has reached a natural closure, the leader ends the session. The leader thanks the students for being part of the Sharing Circle and states that it is over.

What follows is a more detailed look at the process of leading a Sharing Circle.

Steps for Leading a Sharing Circle

1. Welcome Sharing Circle members

2. Review the Sharing Circle rules*

3. Introduce the topic

4. Sharing by circle members

5. Ask discussion questions

6. Close the circle

*optional after the first few sessions

1. Welcome Sharing Circle members

As you sit down with the students in a Sharing Circle group, remember that you are not teaching a lesson. You are facilitating a group of people. Establish a positive atmosphere. In a relaxed manner, address each student by name, using eye contact and conveying warmth. An attitude of seriousness blended with enthusiasm will let the students know that this Sharing Circle group is an important learning experience—an activity that can be interesting and meaningful.

2. Review the Sharing Circle rules

At the beginning of the first Sharing Circle, and at appropriate intervals thereafter, go over the rules for the circle. They are:

Sharing Circle Rules

- Everyone gets a turn to share, including the leader.

- You can skip your turn if you wish.

- Listen to the person who is sharing.

- There are no interruptions, probing, put-downs, or gossip.

- Share the time equally.

From this point on, demonstrate to the students that you expect them to remember and abide by the ground rules. Convey that you think well of them and know they are fully capable of responsible behavior. Let them know that by coming to the Sharing Circle they are making a commitment to listen and show acceptance and respect for the other students and you. It is helpful to write the rules on chart paper and keep them on display for the benefit of each Sharing Circle session.

3. Introduce the topic

State the topic, and then in your own words, elaborate and provide examples as each lesson in this book suggests. The introduction or elaboration of the topic is designed to get students focused and thinking about how they will respond to the topic. By providing more than just the mere statement of the topic, the elaboration gives students a few moments to expand their thinking and to make a personal connection to the topic at hand. Add clarifying statements of your own that will help the students understand the topic. Answer questions about the topic, and emphasize that there are no "right" responses. Finally, restate the topic, opening the session to responses (theirs and yours). Sometimes taking your turn first helps the students understand the aim of the topic. The introductions, as written in this book, are provided to give you some general ideas for opening the Sharing Circle. It's important that you adjust and modify the introduction and elaboration to suit the ages, abilities, levels, cultural/ethnic backgrounds and interests of your students.

4. Sharing by circle members

The most important point to remember is this: The purpose of these Sharing Circles is to give students an opportunity to express themselves and be accepted for the experiences, thoughts, and feelings they share. Avoid taking the action away from the students. They are the stars!

5. Ask discussion questions

Responding to discussion questions is the cognitive portion of the process. During this phase, the leader asks thought-provoking questions to stimulate free discussion and higher-level thinking. Each Sharing Circle lesson in this book concludes with several discussion questions. At times, you may want to formulate questions that are more appropriate to the level of understanding in your students— or to what was actually shared in the circle. If you wish to make connections between the topic and your content area, ask questions that will accomplish that objective and allow the answering of the discussion questions to extend longer. We have left a space on each page for you to note significant other questions that you create and find effective.

6. Close the circle

The ideal time to end a Sharing Circle is when the discussion question phase reaches natural closure. Sincerely thank everyone for being part of the circle. Don't thank specific students for speaking, as doing so might convey the impression that speaking is more appreciated than mere listening. Then close the group by saying, "This Sharing Circle is over," or "OK, that ends our circle."

More about Sharing Circle Steps and Rules

The next few paragraphs offer further clarification concerning leadership of Sharing Circles.

Who gets to talk? Everyone. The importance of acceptance cannot be overly stressed. In one way or another practically every ground rule says one thing: accept one another. When you model acceptance of students, they will learn how to be accepting. Each individual in the group is important and deserves a turn to speak if he or she wishes to take it. Equal opportunity to become involved should be given to everyone in the Sharing Circle.

Members should be reinforced equally for their contributions. There are many reasons why a leader may become more enthused over what one student shares than another. The response may be more on target, reflect more depth, be more entertaining, be philosophically more in keeping with one's own point of view, and so on. However, students need to be given equal recognition for their contributions, even if the contribution is to listen silently throughout the session.

In most of the Sharing Circles, plan to take a turn and address the topic, too. Students usually appreciate it very much and learn a great deal when their teachers, counselors, and other adults are willing to tell about their own experiences, thoughts, and feelings. In this way you let your students know that you acknowledge your own humanness.

Does everyone have to take a turn? No. Students may choose to skip their turns. If the circle becomes a pressure situation in which the members are coerced in any way to speak, it will become an unsafe place where participants are not comfortable. Meaningful discussion is unlikely in such an atmosphere. By allowing students to make this choice, you are showing them that you accept their right to remain silent if that is what they choose to do.

As you begin the circle, it's important to remember that it's not a problem if one or more students decline to speak. If you are imperturbable and accepting when this happens, you let them know you are offering them an opportunity to experience something you think is valuable, or at least worth a try, and not attempting to force-feed them. You as a leader should not feel compelled to share a personal experience in every session, either. However, if you decline

to speak in most of the sessions, this may have an inhibiting effect on the students' willingness to share.

A word should also be said about how this ground rule has sometimes been carried to extremes. Sometimes leaders have bent over backwards to let students know they don't have to take a turn. This seeming lack of enthusiasm on the part of the leader has caused reticence in the students. In order to avoid this outcome, don't project any personal insecurity as you lead the session. Be confident in your proven ability to work with students. Expect something to happen and it will.

Some leaders ask the participants to raise their hands when they wish to speak, while others simply allow free verbal sharing without soliciting the leader's permission first. Choose the procedure that works best for you, but do not call on anyone unless you can see signs of readiness. And do not merely go around the circle.

Some leaders have reported that their first group fell flat—that no one, or just one or two students, had anything to say. But they continued to have groups, and at a certain point everything changed. Thereafter, the students had a great deal to say that these leaders considered worth waiting for. It appears that in these cases the leaders' acceptance of the right to skip turns was a key factor. In time most students will contribute verbally when they have something they want to say, and when they are assured there is no pressure to do so.

Sometimes a silence occurs during a session. Don't feel you have to jump in every time someone stops talking. During silences students have an opportunity to think about what they would like to share or to contemplate an important idea they've heard. A general rule of thumb is to allow silence to the point that you observe group discomfort. At that point move on. Do not switch to another topic. To do so implies you will not be satisfied until the students speak. If you change to another topic, you are telling them you didn't really mean it when you said they didn't have to take a turn if they didn't want to.

If you are bothered about students who attend a number of sessions and still do not share verbally, reevaluate what you consider to be involvement. Participation does not necessarily mean talking. Students who do not speak are listening and learning.

How can I encourage effective listening? The Sharing Circle is a time (and place) for students and leaders to strengthen the habit of listening by doing it over and over again. No one was born knowing how to listen effectively to others. It is a skill like any other that gets better as it is practiced. In the immediacy of the

Sharing Circle the members become keenly aware of the necessity to listen, and most students respond by expecting it of one another.

In these Sharing Circles, listening is defined as the respectful focusing of attention on individual speakers. It includes eye contact with the speaker and open body posture. It eschews interruptions of any kind. When you lead a circle, listen and encourage listening in the students by (1) focusing your attention on the person who is speaking, (2) being receptive to what the speaker is saying (not mentally planning your next remark), and (3) recognizing the speaker when she finishes speaking, either verbally ("Thanks, Shirley") or nonverbally (a nod and a smile).

To encourage effective listening in the students, reinforce them by letting them know you have noticed they were listening to each other and you appreciate it.

How can I ensure the students get equal time? When group members share the time equally, they demonstrate their acceptance of the notion that everyone's contribution is of equal importance. It is not uncommon to have at least one dominator in a group. This person is usually totally unaware that by continuing to talk he or she is taking time from others who are less assertive. An important social skill is knowing how you affect others in a group and when dominating a group is inappropriate behavior.

Be very clear with the students about the purpose of this ground rule. Tell them at the outset how much time there is. When it is your turn, always limit your own contribution. If someone goes on and on, do intervene (dominators need to know what they are doing), but do so as gently and respectfully as you can.

What are some examples of put-downs? Put-downs convey the message, "You are not okay as you are." Some put-downs are deliberate, but many are made unknowingly. Both kinds are undesirable in a Sharing Circle because they destroy the atmosphere of acceptance and disrupt the flow of sharing and discussion. Typical put-downs include:

- over questioning.
- statements that have the effect of teaching or preaching
- advice giving
- one-upsmanship
- criticism, disapproval, or objections
- sarcasm
- statements or questions of disbelief

How can I deal with put-downs?
There are two major ways for dealing with put-downs: preventing them from occurring and intervening when they do.

Going over the rules with the students at the beginning of each Sharing Circle, particularly in the earliest sessions, is a helpful preventive technique. Another is to reinforce the students when they adhere to the rule. Be sure to use non patronizing, non evaluative language.

Unacceptable behavior should be stopped the moment it is recognized by the leader. When you become aware that a put-down is occurring, do whatever you ordinarily do to stop destructive behavior. If one student gives another an unasked-for bit of advice, say for example, "Jane, please give Alicia a chance to tell her story." To a student who interrupts say, "Ed, it's Sally's turn." In most cases the fewer words, the better—students automatically tune out messages delivered as lectures.

Sometimes students disrupt the group by starting a private conversation with the person next to them. Touch the offender on the arm or shoulder while continuing to give eye contact to the student who is speaking. If you can't reach the offender, simply remind him or her of the rule about listening.

If students persist in putting others down or disrupt the circle, ask to see them at another time and hold a brief one-to-one conference, urging them to follow the rules. Suggest that they reconsider their membership in the group. Make it clear that if they don't intend to honor the rules, they are not to come to the group.

How can I keep students from gossiping? Periodically remind students that using names and sharing embarrassing information in a Sharing Circle is not acceptable. Urge the students to relate personally to one another, but not to tell intimate details of their lives.

What should the leader do during the discussion question phase? Conduct this part of the process as an open forum, giving students the opportunity to discuss a variety of ideas and accept those that make sense to them. Don't impose your opinions on the students, or allow the students to impose theirs on one another. Ask open-ended questions, encourage higher-level thinking, contribute your own ideas when appropriate, and act as a facilitator.

In Conclusion: The Two Most Important Things to Remember

No matter what happens in a Sharing Circle session, the following two elements are the most critical:

1. Everyone gets a turn.

2. Everyone who takes a turn gets listened to with respect.

What does it mean to get a turn? Imagine a pie divided into as many pieces as there are people in the group. Telling the students that everyone gets a turn, whether they want to take it or not, is like telling them that each one gets a piece of the pie. Some students may not want their piece right away, but they know it's there to take when they do want it. As the teacher or counselor, you must protect this shared ownership. Getting a turn not only represents a chance to talk, it is an assurance that every member of the group has a "space" that no one else will violate.

When students take their turn, they will be listened to. There will be no attempt by anyone to manipulate what a student is offering. That is, the student will not be probed, interrupted, interpreted, analyzed, put-down, joked-at, advised, preached to, and so on. To "listen to" is to respectfully focus attention on the speaker and to let the speaker know that you have heard what he or she has said.

In the final analysis, the only way that a Sharing Circle can be evaluated is against these two criteria. Thus, if only two students choose to speak, but are listened to—even if they don't say very "deep" or "meaningful" things—the discussion group can be considered a success.

A Time I Felt Happy

Purpose:

To help the students develop a "feeling" vocabulary and to verbalize both positive and negative feelings.

Theme:

Self Awareness

Introducing the Topic:

In your own words, say to the students: *Today we are going to talk about happy feelings in our discussion. Sometimes we feel happy and sometimes we don't—we feel unhappy, but our topic for this session is, "A Time I Felt Happy." Can you remember a time when you felt happy? Maybe something very nice happened and you felt good about it. Or perhaps someone did something for you that you really liked. Perhaps you remember being in a special place and feeling full of joy and energy, or maybe you experienced a happy feeling because you had just accomplished something significant. Take a moment to think about it and when you're ready, the topic is, "A Time I Felt Happy."*

Discussion questions:

— *Why is it good for us to tell one another about times we felt happy?*
— *What similarities and differences did you notice about what makes us happy?*
— *How did it make you feel when you were talking about a happy time?*

Your questions:

A Time I Felt Unhappy

Purpose:

    To help the students develop a "feeling" vocabulary and to verbalize both positive and negative feelings.

Theme:

Self Awareness

Introducing the Topic:

    In your own words, say to the students: *In our last discussion group, we talked about times we felt happy. We learned that in some places, like this group, it's all right for us to tell each other about our feelings. And today we are going to do that again. Our topic for today is, "A Time I Felt Unhappy." Everybody feels happy at times and everybody feels unhappy at other times. It's more fun for most people to tell about happy feelings, but sometimes it does us good to talk about unhappy feelings as well. Can you remember a time when you felt unhappy? Maybe you had an accident and got hurt, or perhaps you wanted something and you didn't get it so you were disappointed. If you would like to take a turn, tell us what made you unhappy and what the feeling was like for you. Take a moment to think about it and when you are ready, the topic is, "A Time I Felt Unhappy."*

Discussion questions:

— *Why is it good for us to tell one another about times we felt unhappy?*
— *What similarities and differences did you notice about what makes us unhappy?*
— *How did it make you feel to remember an unhappy time?*

Your Questions:

A Time I Felt Scared

Purpose:

    To help students understand their thoughts about fear and to recognize that everyone experiences fear at times. This topic also helps students to recognize that there are strategies they can use to manage their fears.

Theme:

    Self Awareness and Self Management

Introducing the Topic:

    In your own words, say to the students: *Everyone feels scared from time to time and no one likes the feeling. Today, we are going to talk about feeling afraid. The topic is, "A Time I Felt Scared." Can you think of a time that you were afraid? What happened to cause your fear? Were you lost? Were you around a lot of people that you didn't know? Was it the first day of school? Perhaps you felt afraid the first time you tried to swim in a pool or the ocean. Chances are there is something that makes you feel scared even now. Are you afraid of the dark? Do big dogs frighten you? Take a moment and think of one time when you felt afraid. When you look toward me, I'll know that you are ready to begin the discussion. The topic is, "A Time I Felt Scared."*

Discussion questions:

—*How do we feel inside when we feel scared?*
—*What do we do sometimes when we are afraid?*
—*Why is it important to talk about our fears?*
—*What are some ways we could lessen our fears or even make them disappear?*

Your questions:

29

A Time I Felt Excited

Purpose:

To help the students to verbalize feelings and to describe emotional experience.

Theme:

Self Awareness

Introducing the Topic:

In your own words, say to the students: *Our topic is, "A Time I Felt Excited."* Explain that everyone gets excited from time to time, for all kinds of reasons, but that people don't all get excited for the same reason. In your own words, say: *Different things or events make us excited. Sometimes it's a birthday, or Christmas, or another holiday, like the Fourth of July. It could be an event like a parade or a party. Does winning a game make you excited? Do you feel excited when you go on afield trip with your class or on a vacation with your family? Would it be exciting for you to go to an amusement or theme park or the zoo? Perhaps you were excited when you got a new baby brother or sister. Think about how you felt physically inside. How did you show that you were excited? Close your eyes and take a few minutes to think quietly about a time when something made you feel excited. When you look up, I'll* know that you are ready to begin the discussion. The topic is, " A Time I Felt Excited."

Discussion questions:

— *What are some of the ways we show that we are excited ?*
— *Why do you think it is important to share the different things that make us excited ?*
— *How do you feel when you're excited?*
— *What are some of your behaviors that show you're excited?*

Your questions:

A Time I Had Fun with a Friend

Purpose:

The students will identify the value of sharing enjoyable activities with friends and recognize cooperative attitudes as being important to relationships.

Theme:

Relationship Skills

Introducing the Topic:

In your own words say to the students: *We all have work to do, both at home and at school. Work is important. But fun and play are important too. Today we're going to talk about having fun. Our topic is, "A Time I Had Fun with a Friend." Think of something fun that you did with a friend. Maybe you and your friend went to a movie together—or to Disney World. Perhaps you played games together. Or maybe you went to your friend's house and played, listened to music or just talked together. Did you share an ice cream with your friend after school? Did you play a video or computer game together? Take a few minutes to think of something you did with a friend that you enjoyed. Look toward me when you are ready to speak. Our topic is, "A Time I Had Fun with a Friend."*

Discussion questions:

— *What kinds of fun things do we do with our friends?*
— *Do our friends have fun doing those things too?*
— *How can you tell if a person is having fun?*
— *Why is it important to do enjoyable things with friends?*
— *What would it be like if we worked all the time and never had fun?*

Your questions

An Activity I Enjoy When I'm by Myself

Purpose:

To help students get in touch with positive feelings and identify strategies and activities they can do to manage moods.

Theme:

Self Awareness and Self Management

Introducing the Topic:

In your own words, say to the students: *We all have things we like to do with others and we also have things we enjoy doing alone. In today's session we're going to discuss things we do when we're alone. The topic is, "An Activity I Enjoy When I'm by Myself." What do you like to do when you're alone? Maybe you enjoy reading or putting puzzles together. Possibly you like to build elaborate constructions or perfect your video-game skills. Maybe you enjoy imagining things or listening to music. Do you write stories or poems, draw pictures, or perform science experiments? Maybe you prefer to be outdoors, riding your skateboard or bicycle, or daydreaming quietly while relaxing in a special place. Think about it for a few moments. Look at me to show that you are ready. The topic is, "An Activity I Enjoy When I'm by Myself."*

Discussion questions:

— *How do the activities we enjoy differ?*
— *Do you think you will still enjoy your activity as an adult? Why or why not?*
— *How do you feel when you are involved in your activity?*
— *If this is an activity you enjoy and feel good when doing, how can you use this knowledge when you have times when you don't feel so good?*

Your questions:

One of the Best Times I Ever Had With My Family

Purpose:

To help students describe positive events and to recognize the value of cooperative activities.

Theme:

Relationship Skills

Introducing the Topic:

In your own words, say to the students: *Our topic today is, "One of the Best Times I Ever Had With My Family." Think about a time when you were with one or more members of your family and everyone had a particularly enjoyable time together. Maybe you visited a roller rink or an amusement park, or took a family trip to a special place. Perhaps you were celebrating someone's birthday, or maybe you all just decided to go to a movie together. It could be a special holiday that your family celebrates in a special way. Tell us what you did with your family, and tell us what made it so enjoyable. Think about it for a moment, and look at me when you are ready to share. Today's topic is, "One of the Best Times I Ever Had With My Family."*

Discussion questions:

— *How did you feel when you went (horseback riding with your family)?*
— *How did other members of your family seem to feel?*
— *Did all of us get the same feelings in the same ways when we had good times with our families?*
— *What differences in feelings and experiences did you notice?*
— *Why is it important to have good times with our families?*

Your questions:

Something I Really Like To Do at School

Purpose:

To help the students to identify interests, abilities, strengths, and weaknesses as components of personal uniqueness and to help them recognize and accept the similarities and differences among others.

Theme:

Self Awareness

Introducing the Topic:

In your own words, say to the students: *Our topic for this discussion is, "Something I Really Like To Do at School." There are so many enjoyable things we do at school. I like practically everything we do, but I do have some favorites. Today I'd like you to think about what you enjoy most here at school. Perhaps you like games because you like moving your body. Maybe you are very good at learning to read. Or perhaps you enjoy our discussion groups most because you get to talk and tell us what's on your mind. Think it over for a few moments and when you are ready to begin, look up at me. The topic is, "Something I Really Like To Do at School."*

Discussion questions:

— *What are some of the similarities you noticed?*
— *What are some of the differences?*
— *Is it okay if the thing you like to do is different from the things others like to do?*

Your questions:

Something I Did (or Made) That I'm Proud Of

Purpose:

To help students to find pride and see themselves in a positive light, to recognize personal strengths and to value effort in accomplishments.

Theme:

Self Awareness and Self Management

Introducing the Topic:

In your own words, say to the students: *Think of something that you did, or made, that you are proud of. It could be that you helped solve a problem for a friend or family member. Or perhaps you made great party invitations, or played with a younger brother or sister so your mom could do something she needed to do. Maybe you baked a batch of cookies without burning a single one. Or maybe you learned how to play your favorite song on the piano without making one mistake. Whatever it was, you feel proud that you were able to do it. Take a moment or two to think of something. The topic is, "Something I Did (or Made) That I'm Proud Of."*

Discussion questions:

— *What kinds of things were we proud of?*
— *What difference is there between being pleased and being proud?*
— *Why is it important to feel pride in our accomplishments?*
— *How can you encourage yourself to do (or make) more things that you will be proud of?*

Your questions:

What I Value Most in a Friend

Purpose:

To help students understand what it takes to get along well with other people and to understand the value of effectively managing emotions in relationships.

Theme:

Relationship Skills

Introducing the Topic:

In your own words, say to the students: *Good friends can be and do many things for each other. I would like you to decide what some of those things are for today's discussion topic, "What I Value Most in a Friend." What do you and your friends say and do to make your friendships work, and to make them special? What qualities do you think are important in a friend? Do you value honesty? ...loyalty? ...listening? ...common interests? ...having time to be together? Think about it for a moment and, when you are ready, our topic is, "What I Value Most in a Friend."*

Discussion questions:

— *What are some of the main qualities that we value in friends?*
— *How do you feel about your friend when he or she does or says something that you think is valuable to the friendship?*
— *If you want your friends to behave in the ways we talked about, would be wise for you to do the same things? Why?*

Your questions:

My Favorite Hero or Heroine

Purpose:

To help students identify a person or character whom they see as heroic and to describe how the accomplishments of their hero relate to their own needs as individuals.

Theme:

Self Awareness

Introducing the Topic:

In your own words, say to the students: *The topic today is, "My Favorite Hero or Heroine." Think about real-life people and fictional characters whom you see as heroes and heroines. Does a real person come to your mind? It might be someone you know personally, such as a member of your family. Or it might be someone whom you know of, like a politician or an entertainer. This hero or heroine might also be someone who is no longer alive, such as a figure from history whom you admire. He or she might even be a fictional character from a movie, TV show, book, or play. Take a minute to think about it. Then, tell us who your favorite fictional or real-life hero or heroine is and what you like and admire about this person. The topic is, "My Favorite Hero or Heroine."*

Discussion questions:

— *What similarities and differences did you notice in the people we think of as heroes and heroines?*
— *Why do people need to have heroes and heroines?*
— *What does your hero or heroine tell you about your own needs, wants, dreams, or goals?*

Your questions:

A Way in Which I'm Responsible

Purpose:

The students will describe responsible behaviors in which they regularly engage to develop an awareness of the value of taking responsibility and following through on commitments.

Theme:

Self Management

Introducing the Topic:

In your own words, say to the students: *The topic for today's discussion is, "A Way in Which I'm Responsible." Think of a responsibility that you accept and carry out. It may be a chore that you do each week, like sweeping the kitchen floor or watering the lawn. Perhaps your responsibility is to do your homework every evening after dinner, or to read a half hour each night before bed. Maybe you get up on time every morning, or fix breakfast for yourself and your younger brothers or sisters. Do you earn and save money? That is a way of being responsible. Before we begin, think quietly for a few moments about something you do that is responsible. The topic is, "A Way in Which I'm Responsible."*

Discussion questions:

— *What are some of the ways in which we are responsible?*
— *What did you learn by hearing about what other students do that is responsible?*
— *Why do you think it is important to have responsibilities?*

Your questions:

Something I Did That Helped Someone Feel Good

Purpose:

To help students to know what their feelings are and to use their feelings to make positive decisions. It also helps develop empathy by examining times when they directly had an impact on someone else's good feelings.

Theme:

Relationship Skills and Self Management

Introducing the Topic:

In your own words, say to the students: *Our topic today is, "Something I Did That Helped Someone Feel Good." We are all affected in some way by the behavior of others toward us. And we have the ability to influence how others feel. Think of a time when you deliberately did something that you knew would trigger a positive reaction in someone. Perhaps your friend was having a bad day and you said something funny that made him or her laugh. Perhaps you did an extra chore at home to help a family member who was feeling overworked. Think of the many things you have done because you wanted someone else to feel good, and share one example with us. Our topic is, "Something I Did That Helped Someone Feel Good."*

Discussion questions:

— *How do you feel when you do something nice for someone else?*
— *How do you benefit by doing something helpful for another person?*
— *When we feel good about ourselves and when we help others, how are we affecting the world we live in?*

Your questions:

How I Help at School

Purpose:

To help students identify personal behaviors required for success in social situations, as well as habits and behaviors that hinder success.

Theme:

Relationship Skills

Introducing the Topic:

In your own words, say to the students: *Everybody has feelings. Sometimes our feelings are nice and sometimes they aren't so nice. Today we are going to talk about things that we do here at school that other people usually like, things that make them feel happy. Our topic is, "How I Help at School." Today, we are going to discuss how we can help out here at school. Think about it. What do you like to do here at school to help? Perhaps what you do helps some friends. Maybe you share things with them. Maybe you help me. Teachers always like it so much when students are helpful. Or maybe you are helpful to yourself. You pay close attention and try to learn as much as you can because you know you are helping yourself when you do that. Tell us one way that you are helpful at school. Let's take a few moments to think it over before we start to share. The topic is, "How I Help at School."*

Discussion questions:

— *What are some of the things we heard about that are helpful to do at school?*
— *Can you think of any other helpful things we can do at school?*
— *Can you think of any things we shouldn't do at school because they are not helpful?*

In the course of the discussion, generate as many ideas as possible about helpful behaviors. Talk about how everyone gains when people help one another. Assist the students to recognize that there are unhelpful behaviors that deserve attention too, behaviors which benefit no one and should be avoided.

Your questions:

A Way I Show I'm a Good Friend

Purpose:

To contribute to an understanding of what it takes to maintain relationships and to understand the elements of give and take.

Theme:

Relationship Skills

Introducing the Topic:

In your own words, say to the students: *Our topic for this session is, "A Way I Show I'm a Good Friend." There are many things we can do to demonstrate that we are a good friend. We can be helpful and supportive all the time, and we can do special things on special occasions. How do you show your friendship? Maybe you show it in the way you handle disagreements, or offer to help when your friend is in a jam. Maybe it's something as simple as being a good listener. Think about the things you do for your friends. When you're ready to share, the topic is, "A Way I Show I'm a Good Friend."*

Discussion questions:

— *What are some similarities and differences in the ways we show we're a good friend?*
— *Why is it important to actively show that you're a good friend?*
— *How do you feel when you are being a good friend?*

Your questions:

A Good Habit I Plan to Keep

Purpose:

To help students consciously identify and reinforce helpful habits and to hear about positive habits and behaviors others employ. The topic also allows students to understand that we can develop positive habits through awareness and self-control.

Theme:

Self Management

Introducing the Topic:

In your own words, say to the students: *In this discussion group, we're going to talk about habits and behaviors. The topic is, "A Good Habit I Plan to Keep." Most of us have both kinds of habits—helpful and not-so-helpful. In this session, we're going to talk about our good ones. Think of a good habit you have, like always greeting people when you see them, or saying thank you when someone does something for you. Maybe you make a habit of feeding your pet every morning, or helping at home in the kitchen every evening or completing your homework before you play or watch TV. Perhaps the habit that comes to your mind is a health habit, like brushing your teeth regularly, eating food that's good for you, or getting lots of exercise. Take a few moments to think about it. When you are ready to share, look at me. The topic is, "A Good Habit I Plan to Keep."*

Discussion questions:

— *How does having a good habit cause you to feel about yourself?*
— *What good habits did you hear about that you'd like to develop?*
— *What's the difference between a good habit and a bad habit?*
— *How would you go about replacing a bad habit with a good habit?*

Your questions:

Someone I'd Like to Be Like

Purpose:

To help students identify a role model and describe the influence that person has on their life.

Theme:

Self Awareness

Introducing the Topic:

In your own words, say to the students: *Our topic for this session is, "Someone I'd like to Be Like." You've all heard the term "model." When you hear it, you probably think of a photographer's model or a fashion model. Or maybe you think of a model airplane, car, or train. There's another meaning for the word model. It means anyone who shows us how to act or how to do something. Parents and teachers are models, and so are you when others watch what you do and model your behavior. This session offers us a chance to talk about our own models. Do you know an older teenager, a young adult, or an older adult whom you look up to? This is someone you probably find yourself imitating. It might be someone you know personally, like an older brother, sister, cousin, or neighbor. Or it might be someone you don't know personally, like a TV star or a sports figure. Think about it for a minute. Then tell us about a person who is a model for you. The topic is, "Someone I'd Like to Be Like."*

Discussion questions:

— *What characteristics did our models have in common?*
— *What causes you to choose one role model and not another?*
— *Is it possible to learn how not to be from certain models? Explain.*
— *What positive attribute does your model demonstrate that you would like to have?*

Your questions:

43

A Talent I'd Like to Develop

Purpose:

To help students get in touch with positive feelings and desires and to use these to make good decisions in life.

Theme:

Self Awareness and Self Management

Introducing the Topic:

In your own words, say to the students: *Our topic for this session is, "A Talent I'd Like to Develop." Is there a special talent or ability that you wish you could develop? Do you ever daydream about being a heart surgeon, a country western singer, a great gymnast, or a soap opera star? Maybe the talent you want to develop is one that you already possess, or maybe you just wonder sometimes what it would be like to have this ability. The talent could be in any area—art, music, science, dance, athletics, etc. Take a minute or two to think it over. The topic is, "A Talent I'd Like to Develop."*

Discussion questions:

— *Is talent something we're born with or something we develop?*
— *If you really want to develop the talent you told us about, how could you get started?*
— *Do you think most adults who are famous for their talents knew what those talents were when they were your age? How do you suppose they discovered them?*

Your questions:

Something That Really Made Me Angry

Purpose:

To help students understand their feelings and examine their thoughts and actions.

Theme:

Self Awareness and Self Management

Introducing the Topic:

In your own words, say to the students: *Our topic for this session is, "Something That Really Made Me Angry. Think of a time something made you angry—a time that you'd feel OK telling us about. It could be a time when someone treated you unfairly, or a time that you were angry with yourself for breaking or losing something you liked. Or perhaps you were mad because you couldn't do something you wanted to do. It can be anything big or small that made you mad. Let's take a few quiet moments to think it over, and when sharing, please don't use any names. The topic is, "Something That Really Made Me Angry."*

Discussion questions:

— *How do our bodies react when we are angry?*
— *What purpose, if any, does getting angry serve?*
— *What are some things we can do when we are angry to change how we are feeling?*

Your questions:

A Time When I Accepted Someone Else's Feelings

Purpose:

To afford students an opportunity to see themselves in giving and nurturing roles and to recognize how they can benefit from this kind of interaction

Theme:

Relationship Skills

Introducing the Topic:

In you own words, say to the students: *As we all know, it means a lot to each of us to have our feelings accepted. When someone accepts your feelings, it's the same as accepting you. In this session we are going to turn this idea around and talk about how it feels to be accepted. The topic is "A Time When I Accepted Someone Else's Feelings." Can you remember a time when you gave attention to someone else and accepted his or her feelings? Keep in mind that this may mean accepting feelings that are different from your own, without getting angry or judging the person. So tell us, if you wish, about a time you did this. The topic is, "A Time When I Accepted Someone Else's Feelings."*

Discussion questions:

— *Is it easy to accept someone else's feelings?*
— *Are there times when people do not accept other's feelings and do not know why?*
— *Can you accept someone else's feelings without compromising your own?"*

Your questions:

When Someone Wouldn't Accept My Point of View

Purpose:

To allow students to discuss the frustration one generally feels when his/her viewpoint is discounted and to develop an awareness that there are many ways to see and respond to all life events. The legitimacy of each person's reality is a focal point of this activity.

Theme:

Relationship Skills

Introducing the Topic:

In your own words, say to the students: *Our topic for this session is "When Someone Wouldn't Accept My Point of View." Can you think of a time like this—when you saw things a certain way, and as far as you were concerned, your view point was right, but someone else wouldn't accept your viewpoint? The disagreement may have been about something you saw happen, or maybe it had to do with an opinion you held or a feeling you had. Maybe you were taught to think or behave a certain way and someone else didn't understand. Maybe the other person was very offensive about it and said you were wrong. Or perhaps the person's facial expression told you your opinion didn't count. Take a minute to think about it, and tell us about what happened, but remember not use any names. The topic is "When Someone Wouldn't Accept My Point of View."*

Discussion questions:

— *How do you feel when someone discounts your point of view?*
— *Even if you don't agree, is it important to allow someone else the right to have their own point of view? Why?*
— *What do you think causes people to reject other people's points of view?*
— *People who think they are always right may win arguments, but do you think they lose anything? If so, what?*

Your questions:

How the Members of My Family Support and Help One Another

Purpose:

To help students describe the interdependence of the family unit in terms of working together and sharing responsibilities and to identify helpful, cooperative activities.

Theme:

Relationship Skills

Introducing the Topic:

In your own words, say to the students: *Our topic today is, "How the Members of My Family Support and Help One Another." A characteristic of families that we sometimes take for granted is that family members are constantly helping one another. We do many big and small things for each other every day. Think of an example of how one member of your family helps another. Maybe your dad helps your brother or sister with homework, or your mom drives your grandmother to her appointments with the doctor. Possibly your older brother or sister occasionally plays your favorite game with you or helps you put together a tough puzzle. Did your parents ever help someone in the family who needed money for an emergency? Who do members of your family talk to when they have a problem? Take a few moments to think about it. When you* have thought of something to share, look at me to show that you are ready. The topic is, "How the Members of My Family Support and Help One Another."

Discussion questions:

— Why do family members help one another?
— What can happen to a family member who is seldom willing to help others?
— Is it okay to ask for help when you need it? Why or why not?

Your questions:

A Place Where I Feel Safe

Purpose:

To help students identify components of a secure, trust-building environment and to understand the value such a place has in their lives.

Theme:

Self Awareness

Introducing the Topic:

In your own words, say to the students: *Our topic for this session is, "A Place Where I Feel Safe." We have all experienced the feeling of being in a place where we feel good. Often, one of the main reasons we feel good is that , for some personal reason, the environment feels safe. Can you think of a place where you almost always experience a feeling of safety? Maybe you feel safe in your home, or almost anywhere provided you are in the company of a particular person. Perhaps you feel safe when you are with a certain group of friends, or tucked under the covers of your own bed. The safety you feel may come from the place itself, or the person or people, you are with. Take a minute to think about your own experiences and see if there's a place like this for you. The topic is, "A Place Where I Feel Safe."*

Discussion questions:

— *How do you feel when you're in a place where you feel safe?*
— *What features or qualities does this place have that cause you to feel safe?*
— *Do you think it's important foe everyone to have a place where they feel safe?*
— *What features or qualities would make a place unsafe for you?*
— *Does this discussion group feel like a safe place? Why or why not?*

Your questions:

A Time I Knew I Could Do It

Purpose:

This topic helps students examine their thoughts as they led to action and a positive outcome. It also lets them feel pride and see themselves in a positive light.

Theme:

Self Management

Introducing the Topic:

In your own words, say to the students: *Our topic for this session is, "A Time I Knew I Could Do It." Sometimes we just know we can do something. We don't doubt it at all. Think of a time when you felt confident that you could do something. It might have been that you knew you could master a new dance step, pass a test, sink a basket, or get your room clean before you went to the movies. It could have been something quick and easy that required limited effort, or something more difficult. Whatever it was, you knew you could do it—and you were right. Take a few moments to think it over, and remember, "A Time I Knew I Could Do It."*

Discussion questions:

— *How did you know that you could do the thing you shared?*
— *Do you think you could do the same thing again? Why or why not?*
— *How does knowing you could (Pass the test) help you accomplish other things?*

Your questions:

A Time I Disappointed Someone

Purpose:

To help students to examine their actions and understand their consequences. It also helps develop an understanding of other's concerns and feelings and the ability to take another's perspective.

Theme:

Relationship Skills and Self Management

Introducing the Topic:

In your own words, say to the students: *Our topic today is, "A Time I Disappointed Someone." Different people expect different things from us. Sometimes we know we are going to disappoint someone and it cannot be avoided. Sometimes we don't want to, hope we won't, and do anyhow. There are lots of ways to disappoint someone. Think of an example from your life. Your parent might have expected you to complete a task and you didn't. A friend might have expected you to go to the movies and you couldn't. Sometimes you might even disappoint yourself! You might have expected to get an A on a book report you wrote, and then discovered that you got only a C. Maybe you told a small lie and got caught. Close your eyes and think for a moment of a time when you heard those words, "I'm disappointed in you." When you're ready, our topic for discussion is, "A Time I Disappointed Someone."*

Discussion questions:

— *How do you feel when you disappoint someone?*
— *What is the relationship between expectation and disappointment?*
— *What can you do about someone's disappointment in you?*

Your questions:

Something I Like About One of My Best Friends

Purpose:

To help students realize that understanding their feelings and desires can help them make good decisions and to help students develop effective social skills.

Theme:

Relationship Skills

Introducing the Topic:

In your own words, say to the students: *The topic for our discussion today is, "Something I Like About One of My Best Friends." Most of us have several close friends, or "best" friends. Think about one of the things that you especially like about one of your best friends. Is it how he treats you? Could it be that she walks home from school with you everyday? Perhaps your friend is funny, or helps you with your spelling. Maybe he plays two-square with you at recess. Don't tell us your friend's name, just the special thing that you like about him or her. Let's take a minute to think quietly about it before we share. The topic is, "Something I Like About One of My Best Friends."*

Discussion questions:

— *What kinds of feelings did you experience as you were sharing about your best friend?*
— *How can we express the positive things we feel about our friends?*
— *How can knowing what you value in a friend help you in choosing and meeting new friends in the future?*
— *Why is it important to think about what we like in a friend?*

Your questions:

Something I Do to Keep a Friend

Purpose:

To help students learn skills for getting along with others and for developing an understanding of what others want and need in relationships.

Theme:

Relationship Skills

Introducing the Topic:

In your own words, say to the students: *Our topic for today's session is, "Something I Do to Keep a Friend." We all have new friends and old friends. What is it that we do to keep a friend for a long time? Think about one of the things you do to make certain that someone will keep choosing you as his or her friend. Are you kind to him? Do you spend time together after school? Do you invite him to ride his bike with you to the park on Saturdays? Maybe you help him or her practice the multiplication tables. Perhaps you share your candy with her when you buy some. Think quietly about it for a few moments before we start. The topic is, "Something I Do to Keep a Friend."*

Discussion questions:

— *Why is it important to work at keeping friendships alive?*
— *What would happen if you didn't do anything to keep your friendships going?*
— *Why is it helpful for us to think of something that we do to keep a friend?*

Your questions:

Something I Like About My Friend Who Is Different

Purpose:

To provide an opportunity for the students to demonstrate respect for and understanding of differences among people, cultures, lifestyles, attitudes, and abilities.

Theme:

Relationship Skills

Introducing the Topic:

In your own words, say to the students: *Today, we are going to talk about a friend who is different from us and what we like about him or her. The topic for this Session is "Something I Like About My Friend Who Is Different." We are all alike and different in many ways. Today I want you to think about a friend who is different from you in at least one way— and why you like this person so much. Your friend might have a different size family than you, or be older than you. Does your friend speak a different language or eat different foods than you? Maybe your friend celebrates birthdays in a different way than you do, or has different holidays. What makes you like your friend so much? Does he or she play with you or share things with you? Invite you to birthday celebrations? Sit down and read with you? Think about it for a few minutes.*

The topic is, "Something I Like About My Friend Who Is Different."

If necessary, give additional examples of differences in physical appearance, culture, or ability.

Discussion questions:

— *In what ways are we different from our friends?*
— *Why do we like our friends even though they are different from us?*
— *Why is it helpful for us to remember what we like about our friends?*
— *How are our lives made better and more exciting by having friends who are different from us?*
— *Do we learn things from people who are different from us? How?*

Your questions:

Something Worth Saving For

Purpose:

To allow students to develop an understanding of how they can use their feelings to make good decisions in life.

Theme:

Self Management

Introducing the Topic:

In your own words, say to the students: *Our topic for this session is, "Something Worth Saving For." When you save money, obviously that means you can't spend it — at least not for awhile. So it helps to know that what you're saving for is really worth giving up some of your spending power. What do you think is valuable enough to save for? A college education? A special trip? A computer or stereo? A car? It doesn't matter if you are actually saving or not. Just think of something important enough to save for and tell us how you would do it. The topic is, "Something Worth Saving For."*

Discussion questions:

— *What are the advantages of saving money? What are the disadvantages?*
— *Why is saving money sometimes so difficult?*
— *What is it like to wait for something you want very much?*
— *How will it feel to finally get the thing for which you have been saving?*

Your questions:

A Time Someone Called Me A Name

Purpose:

To help students develop empathy by becoming more aware of how it feels to others, as well as themselves, to be called names and that some ways of handling these situations are better than others.

Theme:

Relationship Skills and Self Management

Introducing the Topic:

In your own words, say to the students: *The topic for today is "A Time Someone Called Me A Name" For most of us this is not a pleasant topic upon which to think about. However, it is important that we understand what happens when we call someone bad names. We've all seen examples of name-calling in our lives. In fact, it isn't uncommon for us to see it daily in school. Today, see if you can think of a time when someone called you a name. It might have been a situation in which someone was teasing you. Perhaps they referred to your physical coordination, intelligence, physical appearance, or cultural group. Focus on the situation and tell us what it looked like to you, how you felt at the time, and how you reacted to it. Please remember not to mention anybody's name. When you're ready, look my way. The topic is "A Time Someone Called Me a Name."*

Discussion questions:

— *How do you feel when someone calls you a name?*
— *When someone calls you a name, are there any thoughts you can have so it doesn't hurt so much?*
— *How do you feel when you call someone else a name?*
— *What did you learn in this session?*

Your questions:

Something I Accomplished That Really Pleased Me

Purpose:

To allow students to describe specific accomplishments from which they derived pleasure and to understand what motivates them to accomplishment.

Theme:

Self Awareness and Self Management

Introducing the Topic:

In your own words, say to the students: *In the discussion group today, you're going to have a chance to tell us about something you did that you felt particularly good about. The topic is, "Something I Accomplished That Really Pleased Me." Maybe you got an "A" on a special report or project. Perhaps you planted something that bloomed and was beautiful. Maybe you rearranged your room, or taught someone how to do something. Whatever it was, you felt happy when you accomplished it. It's okay if the thing you tell us about was pleasing to someone else, but it must also have been pleasing to you. Think about it for a moment or two, and look at me when you're ready. The topic is, "Something I Accomplished That Really Pleased Me."*

Discussion questions:

— *What was it about your accomplishment that was most pleasing?*
— *What feelings were common to most of us who shared?*
— *Why is it important to find pleasure in the things we accomplish?*
— *Does putting lost of time and effort into an accomplishment bring more pleasure from it? Why?*

Your questions:

A Time I Won and Loved It

Purpose:

To help students recognize their feelings and to understand the relationship between feelings, thoughts and behaviors>

Theme:

Self Awareness

Introducing the Topic:

In your own words, say to the students: *The topic for this session is, "A Time I Won and Loved It." Each of us has had the experience of winning, of tasting victory, of overcoming difficult situations. Think of a time when you did something that caused you to feel like a winner! Maybe you won a game or athletic contest, or perhaps you showed a lot of courage and accomplished something that made you feel very proud. Maybe you won a prize or an award, were elected to a class office, or got the highest grade on a test. Take a minute to think about a time when you were the winner and felt wonderful about it. The topic is, "A Time I Won and Loved It."*

Discussion questions:

— *What kinds of feelings do you have when you win?*
— *What were your thoughts in response to this "winning" experience?*
— *Did you do anything in response to this experience?*
— *Do other people have to lose in order for you to feel like a winner? Why or why not?*
— *What are some situations in which everyone can be a winner?*

Your questions:

A Time I Lost and Took It Hard

Purpose:

To help students in observing themselves and to recognize the relationship between feelings, thoughts and behaviors and also to discuss the dynamics of losing and why it is so difficult.

Theme:

Self Awareness

Introducing the Topic:

In your own words, say to the students: *Our topic for this session is, "A Time I Lost and Took It Hard." Maybe you'll have to think about this one a little bit, or possibly something has already popped into your head. Think of a time when you wanted very much to win at something. You may have worked hard at it, and put all your hopes into it, but you lost. And you felt very badly. Maybe you tried out for a play, a team, or a cheerleading squad. Or maybe you studied hard for a test and thought you had all the answers. Maybe you entered a contest or a race for a class office, but somebody else won instead of you. You may tell us about something that happened recently or a long time ago. Take a minute to think about it and, if you will, tell us about, "A Time I Lost and Took It Hard."*

Discussion questions:

— *How does losing make you feel?*
— *What kind of thoughts did you have in response to this experience?*
— *Did you do anything in response to this experience?*
— *What makes certain losses particularly difficult to take?*
— *When does winning become too important to people?*

Your questions:

Someone Whose Friendship I Value

Purpose:

To help students describe qualities that are of value in maintaining relationships and to learn skills for building trust in relationships.

Theme:

Relationship Skills

Introducing the Topic:

In your own words, say to the students: *Our topic today is, "Someone Whose Friendship I Value." When something is valuable to us, that usually means that it is worth a lot, and that it would be hard to replace. We value things, like bikes, cassette players, and clothing. But we also value people. Think of someone whose friendship you value. Friendship with this person is worth so much to you that it would be hard to replace. Your friend could be someone you see at school, or someone who lives in your neighborhood. He or she could be an older person who takes you special places. Perhaps your friend is someone who teaches you a sport or other skill. Your friend might be a relative, like a brother or sister. It could even be a pet. Tell us who your friend is and what kinds of things you do with your friend. Think about it for a few moments. The topic is, "Someone Whose Friendship I Value."*

Discussion questions:

— *How do we know when we value something or someone?*
— *What kinds of things make a friendship valuable?*
— *Why is it important to know what we value?*

Your questions:

A Way I Show Respect for Others

Purpose:

To help students describe specific behaviors that demonstrate respect for others.

Theme:

Relationship Skills

Introducing the Topic:

In your own words, say to the students: *The topic for this discussion is, "A Way I Show Respect for Others." There are many ways that we can show respect for other people. Tell us about a way that you frequently use. Maybe you remember to say please and thank you, or try never to interrupt others when they're talking, or hold doors when you go through them so they won't swing back and smack the people behind you. Perhaps you try not to say critical things about others, or maybe you listen respectfully to the opinions of people you disagree with. Tell us what you do that is respectful, and how you learned to do it. Think about it for a few moments. The topic is, "A Way I Show Respect for Others."*

Discussion questions:

— *How do you feel about yourself when you show respect for others?*
— *If you want to be respected, will showing respect for others help? How?*
— *Should we show respect for people we don't like? Explain.*

Your questions:

A Time Someone Ruined It for Everyone

Purpose:

To develop an understanding of the value of cooperation in any group setting. This topic also develops an awareness of the fact that feelings affect actions and actions have consequences.

Theme:

Relationship Skills

Introducing the Topic:

In your own words, say to the students: *Today the topic for our discussion session is, "A Time Someone Ruined It for Everyone." Have you ever been with a group when someone did something to ruin the experience for everyone else? Maybe someone in your class shouted out when you were lining up for recess, and the whole class had to stay inside for an extra five minutes. Perhaps someone ruined a birthday party by starting a fight over the biggest piece of cake. Have you ever been to a family outing at which someone started crying or throwing a tantrum, so you all had to go home? Don't mention any names, but tell what the person did to spoil the event for everyone else. Let's quietly give it some thought for a minute. The topic is, "A Time Someone Ruined It for Everyone."*

Discussion questions:

— *How did you feel when someone ruined it for everyone else?*
— *Why is it important to remember that one person's behavior can affect the whole group?*

Your questions:

When Someone Made Me Feel Like a Part of the Group

Purpose:

This topic fosters the development of empathy by helping students recognize that feeling like a stranger or outsider is not uncommon, that being included can be a very positive experience, and that they can help others feel welcome too.

Theme:

Relationship Skills

Introducing the Topic:

In your own words, say to the students: *Today our topic is "When Someone Made Me Feel Like a Part of the Group." Most of us have had the experience of being an "outsider." Usually this happens when we are new to an area or school, or when we are around new people. Most of us probably don't like the uncomfortable feeling of being left out and want to be "In." Sometimes someone in the group will get to know us and bring us inside. That person is the ticket to being "in." Think about a time this happened to you. Maybe it was in a club or at a dance. Perhaps it was a new neighborhood or school. Someone took the time to make you feel welcome and wanted. Our topic is "A Time Someone Made Me Feel Like a Part of the Group."*

Discussion questions:

— *What kind of behaviors help people feel accepted?*
— *How would you go about helping someone feel like part of your group?*
— *When members feel like part of a group or organization, how does it affect the group?*

Your questions:

A Time My Friends Wanted Me to Do Something I Didn't Want to Do

Purpose:

To give students the opportunity to examine and discuss their feelings in response to peer pressures and to understand what it takes to make positive, healthy decisions.

Theme:

Self Management

Introducing the Topic:

In your own words, say to the students: *Today our topic is "A Time My Friends Wanted Me to Do Something I Didn't Want to Do." It is not unusual for friends to want us to join them at something we don't want to do. Sometimes it's as simple as going to a dance or the show when we're just too tired. Sometimes they want us to do something dangerous or illegal and we really know better. On these occasions it's sometimes easy to say "no" to our friends, but often it is very difficult. Pressure from our friends and other students can make us feel so uneasy that we join their activities even when we don't want to. Think about such a time, and without naming names, share with us "A Time My Friends Wanted Me to Do Something I Didn't Want to Do."*

Discussion questions:

— *How do you think peer pressure works?"*
— *What are some ways we can learn to say "no" when it's in our best interest?*
— *How will developing the ability to say "no" help you become a happier, more successful person?*

Your questions:

Something at Which I'm Getting Better

Purpose:

   To give the students a chance to discuss their involvement in something challenging. To help students understand the relationships between success and motivation.

Theme:

   Self Management

Introducing the Topic:

   In your own words, say to the students: *Today we're going to discuss things that we are good at doing and are even improving in. Our topic is, "Something at Which I'm Getting Better." Maybe you've had the experience of learning how to do something lately that takes a long time to do well, such as playing a musical instrument. Or it could be something else you're working on, like speaking English or Spanish, and you've noticed it's getting easier for you. Maybe you decided it's important to control your temper and you're finding that it's getting easier to do that. What ever it might be, think about what you did that helped you to improve, and how it felt when you noticed your improvement? The topic is "Something at Which I 'm Getting Better."*

Discussion questions:

— *How do you feel when you realize you're improving at something?*
— *Why is it important for people to know how well they're doing?"*
— *How can you tell you're improving at something?*
— *When you realize you're improving, does it make you want to improve even more? Why?*

Your questions:

A Time I Felt Left Out

Purpose:

To help students develop empathy for others and learn strategies to be able to manage distressing moods.

Theme:

Relationship Skills

Introducing the Topic:

In your own words, say to the students: *The topic for this session isn't a happy one. It's, "A Time I Felt Left Out." At one time or another, all of us have been left out of something that we wanted to be included in. Maybe it was a game our friends were playing, or a job the family was doing at home, but felt you were too young to participate in. Possibly you weren't feeling well and couldn't go to school on a day everyone else was going on a field trip. Or maybe your friends were invited to a birthday party and you weren't. Whatever it was, you felt left out of what others were doing. Think about it for a few moments and, when you are ready, look at me. The topic is, "A Time I Felt Left Out."*

Discussion questions:

— *How did most of us feel about being left out?*
— *Why is it so important to us to feel included ?*
— *What could you have done to be included ?*
— *What can you do if you see that someone else is being left out?*

Your questions;

What People Like About Me

Purpose:

To help students understand how others are feeling and to describe positive characteristics as perceived by self and others.

Theme:

Self Awareness and Relationship Skills

Introducing the Topic:

In your own words, say to the students: *Today our topic is, "What People Like About Me." Sometimes people tell us what they like about us. What have people told you? Maybe your family likes how helpful you are, or your friends tell you that you have a nice smile. Have people ever told you that they like the way you read or draw? Sometimes you can just tell what a person likes about you, without even being told. Maybe you know that you are appreciated as a friend or a thoughtful brother or sister. Take a few moments to think about it, and when you are ready, we'll begin. The topic is, "What People Like About Me."*

Discussion questions:

— *How does it feel to describe the things that others like about you?*
— *Why is it important to know that others recognize our positive qualities?*
— *Is it okay to ask people what they like best about us? Why or why not?*

Your questions:

Something I Like about Myself

Purpose:

To help students demonstrate a positive attitude and describe positive characteristics about themselves.

Theme:

Self Awareness

Introducing the Topics:

In your own words, say to the students: *Today we are going to talk about something everybody loves to talk about. We will talk about ourselves! We're going to get a chance to say some very good and true things about ourselves. The topic is, "Something I Like about Myself." Think about yourself for a few moments. You have so many good qualities that it may be hard to decide which one to talk about. Maybe you're glad to be yourself because you learn things so easily. Or maybe you are good at playing and having fun with your friends. Perhaps you like something about your body, like your curly hair or your freckles. Maybe you're proud of your ability to play games and sports well. Let's think about it for a moment. When you are ready to share, look at me. The topic is, "Something I Like about Myself."*

Discussion questions:

— *Is it okay for us to say what we like about ourselves in this discussion group?*
— *Why is it good for us to take pride in ourselves?*
— *How do other people let you know that they are proud of you?*

Assure the students that the discussion group is a perfect place for them to say positive things about themselves. Help them to articulate how important it is to like and take pride in themselves.

Your questions:

Something I Like to Do With Other People

Purpose:

To help students to develop an understanding of group dynamics, what it takes to get along with others, and to enhance self-awareness by discussing what brings them pleasure.

Theme:

Relationship Skills and Self Awareness

Introducing the Topic:

In your own words, say to the students: *Today's topic is, "Something I Like to Do With Other People." It's fun to do things with other people. Most games require two or more people, as do many sports, such as football, baseball, even tennis. Think of something you like to do with other people. It might be shopping or talking on the phone. Perhaps you like big family picnics or holiday dinners. Or maybe you enjoy having lunch with friends. Do you have more fun at amusement parks when you are with a group? Think of one thing you like to do with other people and tell us about it. The topic is, "Something I Like to Do With Other People."*

Discussion questions:

— *What do we gain by experiencing events and activities with other people?*
— *What happens when a group gets too large for a particular activity? What are the effects of having too few people?*
— *What are some things you do when you're with others to show you're a good group member?*

Your questions:

When Someone Expected the Very Best of Me

Purpose:

To have students explore ways in which the expectations of others influence their behavior and to develop an understanding of how people persuade or lead others.

Theme:

Self Management and Relationship Skills

Introducing the Topic:

In your own words, say to the students: *Our session for today is all about expectations. The topic is, "When Someone Expected the Very Best of Me." Can you think of a time when you were expected to do your very best at something? This incident may have occurred a long time ago or very recently, and it may involve any kind of situation. You might have been expected to perform well in an athletic event, a game, some kind of project or assignment you were involved in at school, or something you were doing with your friends. The important thing to consider is how you were affected by the person who expected you to do your best. Did you feel good about this person's faith in you, or was the pressure uncomfortable? Maybe you felt both ways at the same time. Take a minute to think it over and, if you will,* tell us what happened and how you felt. The topic for today's session is, "When Someone Expected the Very Best of Me."

Discussion questions:

— How did most of us perform when someone expected us to do well?
— When someone expects a person to do poorly, what generally happens? Why?
— What have you learned about how people influence each other from this session?

Your questions:

I Observed a Conflict

Purpose:

To give students an opportunity to think about and discuss conflicts they have observed in order to build more clearly their understanding of the dynamics of conflicts and, therefore, what it takes to get along with others.

Theme:

Relationship Skills

Introducing the Topic:

In your own words, say to the students: Our topic is, *I Observed a Conflict." There probably isn't anyone here who hasn't at some point in his or her life watched some kind of conflict taking place. Conflicts have many forms—a clash of ideas or needs, a real fight, or an argument involving some kind of physical or verbal violence. Without actually telling us who was involved in the conflict you saw, or your relationship with them, tell us what happened, if you will. The topic is "I Observed a Conflict."*

Discussion questions:

— *Did most of the conflicts we talked about happen in similar ways, and if so, what pattern did you notice?"*
— *What abilities do people seem to lose when they get involved in an upsetting situation?"*
— *What are some things that could have been done to avoid the conflict, or to learn from the conflict?*

Your questions:

How I React When I'm Angry

Purpose:

To allow students to get in touch with a wide range of feelings and to develop an awareness of what is involved in managing distressing moods and how to control impulses.

Theme:

Self Management

Introducing the Topic:

In your own words, say to the students: *Our topic today is, "How I React When I'm Angry." Everybody gets angry. When we get angry, we all have some sort of reaction. Some of us shout, some of us stuff our anger deep inside us, some of us lash out and hit other people or things, and some of us throw and break things. How do you behave when you're angry? Maybe you dive into an activity of some kind and try to keep busy. Perhaps you're one of the many people who handle anger by withdrawing and becoming very silent. Or maybe you react verbally, saying things that you regret later. Think about this for a moment and, if you would like to share, the topic is, "How I React When I'm Angry."*

Discussion questions:

— *What did you learn about handling anger from this discussion topic?*
— *What do you think are the most effective ways of handling anger?*
— *What purpose, if any, does getting angry serve?*

Your questions:

Someone Did Something for Me That I Really Appreciated

Purpose:

To have students explore positive feelings they experienced as a result of someone's kindness and to understand how thoughtful deeds benefit both giver and receiver.

Theme:

Relationship Skills

Introducing the Topic:

In your own words, say to the students: *The topic of this session is, "Someone Did Something for Me That I Really Appreciated." You've probably all been on the receiving end of many thoughtful gestures. Think back over some of those experiences and choose one to share with us. Maybe a friend offered to give you a ride when you needed one, or helped you finish a report that you were struggling with. Perhaps a visiting relative presented you with a special treat, like your favorite cookie, candy, or snack. Or maybe someone listened when you needed to talk about a problem. Think for a moment about something like this that has happened to you. If you told the person how you felt, share that with us, too. The topic for today is, "Someone Did Something for Me That I Really Appreciated."*

Discussion questions:

— *Did you notice any similarities in the kinds of things we appreciated?*
— *How are people able to influence each other's feelings?*
— *Wisdom says that one way to cheer yourself up when you're feeling low is to do something for someone else. What do you think of that idea?*

Your questions:

How I Made Friends and It Turned Out Well

Purpose:

To provide students with valuable information from their peers regarding effective ways to make friends.

Theme:

Relationship Skills

Introducing the Topic:

In your own words, say to the students: *Our topic is "How I Make Friends and It Turned Out Well." Some people have difficulty making friends and some have a knack for doing this easily. Maybe your family moves a lot and you have to make new friends all the time. Can you remember a time when you did this? Perhaps there was someone you liked and wanted for a friend, and you weren't sure how to do it. Were you able to figure out an approach that was successful? Or did you give the matter very little thought? Maybe listening to ways others did it will help all of us get some new ideas for making friends. The topic today is "How I Made Friends and It Turned Out Well."*

Discussion questions:

— *What are some things we do when we want to be friends with someone else?*
— *What were some unusual ways mentioned in this session?*
— *What qualities seem to be essential to making friends?*

Your questions:

Something I Do to Take Care of Myself

Purpose:

To help students to be in touch with positive feelings and to see how good decisions can help them to be happier and healthier.

Theme:

Self Awareness and Self Management

Introducing the Topic:

In your own words, say to the students: *I'm sure most of us like to feel healthy and have plenty of energy. In order to feel good, we need to take care of ourselves. Today's topic is "Something I Do to Take Care of Myself." There are many things we can do to take care of ourselves. The things you do might include going to bed early so you get plenty of sleep, or eating a healthy breakfast in the morning. Maybe you watch your favorite T.V. show because it makes you laugh and feel good. Or maybe you stay quiet and listen to soft music when you don't feel well. Whatever it is that you do for yourself, take a minute to think about it silently before we share. The topic is "Something I Do to Take Care of Myself."*

Discussion questions:

— *Why is it helpful to talk about the ways in which we take care of ourselves?*
— *How do you feel about doing things that are good for you?*
— *What could happen if you didn't take care of yourself?*
— *What have you learned about staying healthy and stress-free?*

Your questions:

I Used Good Judgement

Purpose:

To have students examine their actions and to understand the consequences of good decisions based on sound judgment.

Theme:

Self Management

Introducing the Topic:

In your own words, say to the students: *The topic for this session is, "I Used Good Judgement." The point of this session is to discuss times when our judgement caused us to make choices that worked out well for us. You've used good judgement lots of times. Try to remember an example that you'd feel okay about sharing. Maybe you used good judgment in the way you spent or saved some money. Perhaps you handled a touchy problem extremely well, or asked for help when you needed it. You might have found yourself in a potentially dangerous situation and made choices that preserved your health and/or safety. If you'd like to tell us about a time when you think your judgment was particularly good, we'd like to hear about it. The topic is, "I Used Good Judgement."*

Discussion questions:

— *What similarities did you notice in the things that were told about in this session?*
— *What are we really talking about when we use the term* judgment*?*
— *How do you usually feel when you know that your judgment is sound?*
— *What kinds of pressures or circumstances sometimes cause us to use bad judgment? How can we prevent such things from happening?*

Your questions:

It Was Difficult, but I Controlled Myself

Purpose:

To allow students to explore times in their lives when their ability to use rational self control overruled the need to react impulsively and, therefore, reinforce their awareness and ability to manage impulses.

Theme:

Self Management

Introducing the Topic:

In your own words, say to the students: *The topic for today's session is "It Was Difficult, but I Controlled Myself." See if you can remember a time when you didn't want to, but you controlled yourself. You may have been about to react strongly to some situation without giving your behavior much thought, but were able to gain control of yourself. It might have been a time when someone else said or did something that was very upsetting, but you didn't let it get to you. Maybe you felt you were being treated unfairly or perhaps it was something like being left out of an activity or game. Think it over for a minute and remember not to share any names, just the incident. The topic for this session is "It Was Difficult, but I Controlled Myself."*

Discussion questions:

— *How did you feel about yourself when you were able to use self-control?*
— *Sometimes we make things worse when we say or do something that makes us feel better at the moment. How can we judge when it's best to say or do what we feel like doing, and when its best to use self-control and hold ourselves back?*
— *What are some of the things we can do to maintain self-control during a difficult time?*

Your questions:

Someone in Authority Whom I Respect

Purpose:

To give the students an opportunity to explore the dynamics of positive authority and to identify characteristics that command respect.

Theme:

Relationship Skills

Introducing the Topic:

In your own words, say to the students: *Our topic today is "Someone in Authority Whom I Respect." Does anyone come to mind who is in some kind of authority or leadership position and for whom you have a lot of respect? It may be someone who you know personally who is in some kind of a responsible position. It could be a teacher, parent, or a student who handles his or her leadership position well. Perhaps the person who comes to your mind is someone who holds public office or is a world leader of some kind. Can any of you think of someone like this? Take a minute to think about it. The topic is "Someone in Authority Whom I Respect."*

Discussion questions:

— *Does "respect" mean the same as "like" to you? Explain.*
— *If you were in an authority position, how would you gain respect?*
— *Why is it important for someone in authority to earn the respect of others?*
— *What are some things that can lead to a loss of respect?*

Your questions:

A Time I Was the Leader

Purpose:

To give students a chance to explore their positive and negative feelings about being a leader and to examine what is involved in persuading or leading others.

Theme:

Relationship Skills

Introducing the Topic:

In your own words, say to the students: *Today we're going to talk about "A Time I Was the Leader." Most of you have had one or more experiences with leadership or being in a position of authority. Maybe it was just for a quick minute or a longer period of time. Perhaps you found yourself in an emergency situation in which you had to take charge. Maybe you were the head of a team or a study group or even a group of friends. Or perhaps you were in charge of some small children. There are some very interesting things you might have dealt with or not dealt with as the leader. Sometimes leaders are nervous about leading. Some leaders are good at sharing responsibility with their followers, and others have a hard time knowing how to tell people what to do. Some want the followers to like them so much they forget about leading and just try to be popular. Think of a time you were the leader and share your experience with us. Our topic again is "A Time I Was the Leader."*

Discussion questions:

— *What seem to be the toughest things about being a leader?*
— *What are the advantages and rewards of leadership?*
— *Does a good leader do everything, or does he or she delegate responsibilities to other people?*
— *How did you feel when you were a leader?*

Your questions:

When I Was in a Group of Strangers

Purpose:

To give students the opportunity to explore feelings that go with being in new situations with new people. To help students prepare for the experience of entering unfamiliar social situations.

Theme:

Self Awareness and Relationship Skills

Introducing the Topic:

In your own words, say to the students: *In today's session we're going to think back to a time when we were in a new and possibly strange situation. The topic is "When I Was in a Group of Strangers." Perhaps this is the way you felt when you first started being a member of our discussion group. Maybe this kind of thing has happened to you many times. Maybe you've moved a lot, changed schools, and had to face new situations and new people often. For some people it's easier each time it happens, and for others it isn't. If the situation you think of was one you chose or volunteered for, what was that like? If you knew in advance that you were going to be with this new group, how did it feel when you were thinking about it beforehand? Or maybe you really didn't want to be in the situation, but you had to for some reason. What was that like for you? In either case, did anyone do anything to make you feel more at home, or were you on your own? If you decide to share tell us about the situation and how you felt. The topic is "When I Was in a Group of Strangers."*

Discussion questions:

— What were some of the similar and different feelings expressed in this group.?
— What are the most effective things you can do when you are in a group of strangers?
— What did you learn about making newcomers feel accepted and included in groups you belong to?

Your questions:

A Time I Felt Like I Belonged

Purpose:

To provide students with an opportunity to explore the feelings that go with being accepted and included in a group or activity. They will also be able to explore qualities they possess which help them get along with others.

Theme:

Self Awareness and Relationship Skills

Introducing the Topic:

In your own words, say to the students: *Our topic is "A Time I Felt Like I Belonged" When we talk about belonging to something, it can an organized group or club; it can be a group of friends; perhaps, it's a church group , or a sports team that you play on. It can even be a family group. There are many different kinds of groups. So think of a time you were accepted or included in a group or an activity that was really good for you. How did you get there, and what did it feel like after you were an accepted member? Did someone do something special to give you a comfortable feeling? Maybe you had a secure feeling just because you were with friends or family, or maybe something else about the time and place gave you that feeling. The topic for today is "A Time I Felt Like I Belonged."*

Discussion questions:

— *What does it take to be a good group member?*
— *How does it feel to be accepted by other people?*
— *Do you feel that belonging to a group is important?*
— *What do you do to show others in your group that you value them and the group?*

Your questions:

An Activity I Enjoy Doing with Friends

Purpose:

To help students understand what it takes to get along well with others.

Theme:

Self Awareness and Relationship Skills

Introducing the Topic:

In your own words, say to the students: *Today's topic is, "An Activity I Enjoy with Friends." We all enjoy doing things with our friends. What do you particularly like to do? Maybe you enjoy playing a sport or working on model planes or cars. Perhaps you like to go to the shopping mall with your friends, or watch television. Do you and your friends play video games, or go bicycling or skating? Do you build things out of odds and ends, LEGOS, building blocks, or logs? Do you make up plays and act in them? Whatever it is you most enjoy doing with your friends, please tell us about it. I'll give you a few moments to decide. The topic is, "An Activity I Enjoy Doing with Friends."*

Discussion questions:

— *What kinds of things did most of us enjoy doing with our friends?*
— *Why do we often do different things with different friends?*
— *Who usually decides what you and your friends are going to do? What do you do when you disagree?*

Your questions:

I Almost Got Into a Fight

Purpose:

To help students understand their feelings and to learn skills and strategies to manage their emotions in times of high stress. It also helps students consider ways of dealing with the reactions of others under stress and conflict.

Theme:

Relationship Skills and Self Management

Introducing the Topic:

In your own words, say to the students: *Today we are going to talk about a time when you were so angry with another person that you almost got into a fight. In fact, today's topic is exactly that: "I Almost Got Into a Fight." Each of us has been angry or upset at another person. Sometimes we disagree about something. Other times we are hurt about the way the person has treated us or someone we like. Or the other person thinks that we have done something to hurt him or her. Think of a time when something happened between you and another person that almost caused you to get into a fight. Maybe you were the one who wanted to fight because you were so mad, or perhaps the other person tried to start the fight. Perhaps you both felt like fighting, but you decided not to and tried to get over your angry feelings. Tell us how this happened. Don't mention anyone's name, just say what happened that made you almost start fighting. Close your eyes and think quietly about it. When you look up at me, I'll know that you are ready to begin the discussion. Once again, the topic is, "I Almost Got Into a Fight."*

Discussion questions:

— *How can conflict, or disagreement, lead to good feelings?*
— *What are some ways in which we can keep from getting into a fight,, even if we feel like fighting?*
— *Why do you think it is better to figure out solutions to problems than to fight about them?*

Your questions:

I Have a Friend Who Is Really Different from Me

Purpose:

To give students an opportunity to become more aware of the basic human similarities and the obvious differences in people and to develop an understanding of the importance of respecting differences among people.

Theme:

Relationship Skills

Introducing the Topic:

In your own words, say to the students: *Our topic today is "I Have a Friend Who Is Really Different from Me". Think of a friend of yours with whom you may have a lot in common. Maybe you like to go to the same places for fun, or you like the same kind of music, or you enjoy a sport together, but there is really a big difference between you in some aspect of your lives. Perhaps your friend is of a different race or religion than you, or your backgrounds are different in other cultural ways. Perhaps this good friend is a member of the opposite sex or is younger or older than you. Think about it for a minute. See if you can remember what made this friendship possible. If you decide to share, describe the ways the differences between you and this friend either add to or detract from the friendship. Are there problems as a result of the differences, or do the differences make your relationship more fun and interesting? The topic for today is "I Have a Friend Who Is Really Different from Me."*

Discussion questions:

— *How much do you think differences between people matter in a real relationship?*
— *Do you think there are people with whom we could be friends, who are in some way different from us, whose differences are keeping us from even getting to know each other?*
— *What can we gain by having friends who are different from us?*
— *What would happen if we insisted that all our friends be just like us?*

Your questions:

I Made a Plan and Followed Through

Purpose:

To help students understand that planning helps them follow through and reach their goals.

Theme:

Self Management

Introducing the Topics:

In your own words, say to the students: Our *topic today is, "I Made a Plan and Followed Through." Think of a time when there was something you really wanted to do, and it required some planning on your part. You may have wanted a bike or a stereo, and had to save money to help pay for it. Or maybe you wanted very much to pass a test, or get an "A" in a class—and to do it, you had to plan a study schedule. Possibly you wanted to surprise someone with a party or a gift, and you had to prepare carefully to create the surprise. Whatever it was—your plan succeeded. Take a few moments to think of such a time before we share. The topic is, "I Made a Plan and Followed Through."*

Discussion questions:

— *What was similar about our plans?*
— *What do you think would have happened if no one had made a plan?*
— *Was it helpful to hear about all these plans that succeeded? How?*
— *Did anyone need help to reach his or her goal?*

Your questions:

Something I Chose That Made Me Happy

Purpose:

To help students to examine their decisions and to understand the consequences of those decisions. It also helps students recognize that our feelings are powerful motivators.

Theme:

Self Awareness and Self Management

Introducing the Topic:

In your own words, say to the students: *Our topic for this session is, "Something I Chose That Made Me Happy." Think of a time when you had a choice to make. Maybe you had to choose something you wanted to do, or what clothes you wanted to wear, or a place you wanted to go. The choice could have involved something really special, or just something ordinary, but whatever it was, you were pleased with the results of your choice. Take a moment and think about it. The topic is, "Something I Chose that Made Me Happy."*

Discussion questions:

— *How many different kinds of choices do we make every day?*
— *What are some choices that might have made you unhappy in the situation you shared?*
— *Does thinking about being happy help us make good choices?*

Your questions:

A Hard Choice That I Had to Make

Purpose:

To help students understand that taking responsibility for making hard choices is something we all have to do.

Theme:

Self Management

Introducing the Topic:

In your own words, say to the students: *Our topic for this session is, "A Hard Choice That I Had to Make." Can you think of a choice that you didn't want to make, but had to anyway? Maybe the choice involved something you had to tell someone, or an unpleasant job you had to do. Or perhaps you were going to put off doing something, but decided to go ahead and do it after all. Take some time and think about it. The topic is, "A Hard Choice That I Had to Make."*

Discussion questions:

— *How did you feel when you remembered the hard choice that you made?*
— *Are there times when choosing isn't as hard as we think it will be? Why do you think that is?*

Your questions:

Someone Who Respects My Feelings

Purpose:

To help students recognize the value of feelings and being able to express them freely, and to develop an understanding of how to build trust in relationships.

Theme:

Relationship Skills

Introducing the Topic:

In your own words, say to the students: *Our topic for this session is, "Someone Who Respects My Feelings." Do you know someone who never seems to think that your feelings about things should be any different than they actually are? Someone who never says you shouldn't act mad when you are mad, or happy when you're feeling good—and who never tells you not to cry when you feel sad? This person could be anyone who respects your feelings. Maybe it's an adult in your family, like your mom, dad, or grandparent, or maybe it's some other adult—like someone in your church or neighborhood. Perhaps you have a friend who always respects your feelings. We'd like you to tell us about this person. Describe a time when you were feeling something and he or she respected your feelings. Think it over quietly for a few moments. The topic is, "Someone Who Respects My Feelings."*

Discussion questions:

— *How do you feel about friends who respect your feelings?*
— *What can we learn from people who respect our feelings?*

Your questions:

A Time I Listened Well to Someone

Purpose:

To help students identify the characteristics of good listeners and to develop awareness and skills of good listening.

Theme:

Relationship Skills

Introducing the Topic:

In your own words, say to the students: *The topic for this session is, "A Time I Listened Well to Someone." We've been doing a lot of talking and sharing in our groups, and we have also been listening well to one another. If we hadn't been good listeners, our discussion groups wouldn't have worked. Listening is just as important to communication as talking.*

Can you think of a time when you listened carefully to another person? Perhaps you had a friend who needed to talk about a problem, and you showed you cared by listening and saying very little. Or maybe it was a situation in which you learned a lot from someone who had some interesting and important things to say. Think about times like these, when you used your listening skills, and tell us about one of them.

Let's take a few moments to think it over. The topic is, "A Time I Listened Well to Someone."

Discussion questions:

— *Can you tell if someone is listening to you or not?*
— *When you know someone is listening, how do you feel?*
— *How do you feel when the person you are talking to isn't listening?*
— *What are the things you do to show that you are really listening to someone?*

Your questions:

I Was Afraid, But I Did It Anyway

Purpose:

To help students understand the relationship among feeling, thoughts and behaviors, and to help them find ways to handle fears and other strong emotions in positive ways.

Theme:

Self Management

Introducing the Topic:

In your own words, say to the students: *Our topic for this session is, "I Was Afraid, But I Did It Anyway." Everyone feels afraid sometimes, but there are things we need to do even if we are afraid. Maybe you were afraid the first day of school, but you walked right into class anyway. Have you ever had to go to the doctor and get a shot? You might have been really scared, but you did it anyway. Or perhaps you were afraid of going into the swimming pool to take lessons, but you did it anyway, so you could learn to swim. What about staying home alone? Have the adults in your family ever had to go somewhere and asked you to stay home and wait until they came back? You were scared, but you did it anyway. Think about how you felt inside when you had to do the thing that scared you, and think about how you felt about yourself after you did it. Were you proud? Did you feel better* *because you did it? Think quietly for a few minutes before we share. I'll know you are ready when you look at me. This topic is, "I Was Afraid, But I Did It Anyway."*

Discussion questions:

— *What did you learn by listening to what other students did, even though they were afraid?*
— *Why do you think it is helpful for us to share about times we were afraid?*
— *How does doing something you are afraid to do help you handle fears in the future?*
— *What did you learn from this topic that will help you handle fears in the future?*

Your questions:

How Somebody Hurt My Feelings

Purpose:

This topic provides students the opportunity to observe themselves and to develop skills for managing their feelings and to be able to distinguish between what someone else does or says and their own reactions to someone else.

Theme:

Self Management

Introducing the Topic:

In your own words, say to the students: *Today we are going to talk about, "How Somebody Hurt My Feelings." Our feelings get hurt in many ways. Frequently, we feel hurt because of something that someone else did. The person who hurt us may not even realize the effects of his or her actions. Can you think of a time when someone hurt you? Maybe a friend didn't invite you to a party or ignored you when you wanted to talk. Perhaps someone called you a name, or said something rude to you. Maybe a coach cut you from a team, or a teacher reprimanded you harshly in front of other students. Choose a time when your feelings were hurt. Tell us what happened and how you felt, but please don't mention any names. The topic is, "How Somebody Hurt My Feelings."*

Discussion questions:

— *How does it feel when someone hurts our feelings?*
— *What kinds of things tend to hurt our feelings most?*
— *What are some ways we can cope with hurt feelings?*
— *What role do our expectations play in whether or not we feel hurt?*

Your questions:

I Could Have Hurt Someone's Feelings, But I Didn't

Purpose:

This topic allows students to develop an understanding of others concerns and feelings and to be able to understand their perspectives. It also helps students to get in touch with actions they can take for self management.

Theme:

Relationship Skills and Self Management

Introducing the Topic:

In your own words, say to the students: *Today our topic is, "I Could Have Hurt Someone's Feelings, But I Didn't." We have all been in situations where we could have said or done something to hurt another person. This sort of situation presents itself frequently, for a variety of reasons. Think about a time when you were in this position. Maybe someone said or did something that wasn't appropriate, and you could easily have corrected or criticized the person, but for some reason you decided against it. Perhaps you heard someone exaggerate or lie in order to impress people, but you decided not to let on that you knew the truth. Or when someone made an embarrassing mistake, perhaps you bit your tongue and didn't laugh. Your decision might have been based on friendship, or fear that the person might hurt you back, or your realization that what the person was going through at that moment wasn't easy. Think about an experience you've had like this and, without telling us who the person was, share what happened. Our topic is, "I Could Have Hurt Someone's Feelings, But I Didn't."*

Discussion questions:

— *What were some of the things that kept us from hurting other people's feelings?*
— *How did you feel about yourself for making the choice not to hurt someone's feelings?*
— *What was the most important thing you learned in this session?*

Your questions:

Not a Word Was Spoken, But I Knew How the Person Felt

Purpose:

To help students understand that nonverbal signals are an important part of communication and to identify feelings expressed by nonverbal cues in specific situations.

Theme:

Relationship Skills

Introducing the Topic:

In your own words, say to the students: *Our topic for today is, "Not a Word Was Spoken, But I Knew How the Person Felt." We tend to think we communicate with just the words we speak. However, we also give off clear messages <u>without</u> saying a word. Or we say words, but our bodies say something very different from our words. Think of a time when someone you know didn't say a word, yet you took one look and knew that person was unhappy or angry or delighted or scared. Describe how you think the person felt, and what it was about how the person looked that communicated his or her feelings so clearly. Take a few moments to think it over. The topic is, "Not a Word Was Spoken, But I Knew How the Person Felt."*

Discussion questions:

— *How were you able to tell what the person was feeling without being told?*
— *What were the most obvious clues to the person's feelings?*
— *If you didn't know someone, do you think you could tell how that person was feeling? Why or why not?*
— *Do you think your moods and feelings can be "read" by other people?*

Your questions:

I Didn't Say a Word, But They Knew How I Felt

Purpose:

To help students understand that they communicate through expressions and body language.

Theme:

Relationship Skills

Introducing the Topic:

In your own words, say to the students: *Our topic for today is, "I Didn't Say a Word, But They Knew How I Felt." In the last session, we talked about being able to determine the feelings of others without their telling us. In this session, think of a time when another person, or a group of people, knew how you were feeling, even though you didn't tell them. Maybe you were disappointed, joyful, embarrassed, confused, angry, or thrilled. Whatever the feeling was, someone could see it in you, and told you so. Take a few minutes to think of such a time. The topic is, "I Didn't Say a Word, But They Knew How I Felt."*

Discussion questions:

— *Was it OK, or were you uncomfortable knowing that others could tell how you were feeling?*
— *How do you think the others knew what you were feeling?*
— *What was good about someone's being able to figure out how you felt?*

Your questions:

How I Keep Myself Well

Purpose:

To help students develop a knowledge of good health habits and to manage one's habits for a positive effect.

Theme:

Self Awareness and Self Management

Introducing the Topic:

In your own words, say to the students: *We all like to feel well and have lots of energy. It's no fun to be sick. Today's topic is "How I Keep Myself Well." Sometimes we can't help it when we get sick, but we can do some things to keep ourselves as healthy as possible. Think of something that you do to keep yourself well. Perhaps you wash your hands with soap and water to get the germs off after you use the bathroom. Maybe you eat lots of fruits and vegetables and not very many sweets. Do you brush your teeth after you eat? That's one way you can take care of your health. Do you tell your parents or teacher if you have any pains inside? That's important. Maybe you take a bath or shower everyday. Keeping clean helps you stay healthy. So does exercising when you feel mad inside. Close your eyes for a few moments and think about what you do to keep yourself well. When you have thought of something, open your eyes—then I'll know that you are ready to begin the discussion. The topic is, "How I Keep Myself Well."*

Discussion questions:

— *In what ways do we keep ourselves healthy?*
— *Why do you think it is helpful to talk about how we keep ourselves well?*
— *How can we learn more about staying healthy and stress free?*

Your questions:

I Kept Trying Until I Learned It

Purpose:

To help students gain an understanding of the importance of practice, effort, and learning and to appreciate the value of persistence in reaching a goal.

Theme:

Self Management

Introducing the Topic:

In your own words, say to the students: *Today we are going to talk about learning. Some things are easy to learn and we learn them quickly; however, most of the time, it takes practice and effort to learn something new. We may have to try many times before we do it right. Our topic today is, "I Kept Trying Until I Learned It." Can you think of a time when you tried to learn something and it didn't come easily to you? Maybe you were trying to learn how to skate board or roller blade. Maybe you had new material to learn for a test or a special art project that was difficult to get just right. Whatever it was, it was hard for you and you didn't learn it right away. But you didn't give up either—you kept trying. You worked at it. Think about it for a moment, and when you are ready to share, look at me. The topic is, " I Kept Trying Until I Learned It."*

Discussion questions:

— *Did anyone else have a hard time learning some of the things that were shared? Which ones?*
— *How did you feel when you were trying, but couldn't seem to learn the thing?*
— *How did you feel when you finally learned how to do it?*
— *Did anyone feel like giving up?*
— *What would have happened if you had given up?*

Your questions

How I Helped a Friend Solve a Problem

Purpose:

   To have the students describe and understand ways in which working together cooperatively can overcome problems.

Theme:

   Relationship Skills

Introducing the Topic:

   In your own words, say to the students: *When it comes to solving problems, sometimes two heads are better than one. We're going to talk about times like this in today's session. The topic is, "How I Helped a Friend Solve a Problem." We all get into a jam from time to time and need the help of others. Think of a time when you helped a friend solve a problem that he or she couldn't solve alone. Perhaps your friend wanted to go on a bike ride with the scouts but didn't have a bike, so you lent him yours for the day. Maybe your class got a new student who didn't know anyone, so you were friendly to her and introduced her to others in the room. Have you ever had friends who were angry at each other and had a fight, and you helped them make up? What about a classmate who just couldn't remember the multiplication tables, so you worked with him after school with* flashcards? *Perhaps you helped a friend find her lost dog. Think of a time you helped a friend who was in a jam or had a problem. What kinds of feelings did you have in the situation? I'll give you a few minutes to reflect and come up with something to share. Look at me when you're ready. The topic is, "How I Helped a Friend Solve a Problem."*

Discussion questions:

— *Why do we need to work together to solve problems?*
— *How do you feel when you have helped someone solve a problem?*
— *How can we avoid forcing our help on someone who doesn't want it?*

Your questions:

97

We Worked Together to Get It Done

Purpose:

To help students understand the importance of cooperation in accomplishing a task.

Theme:

Relationship Skills

Introducing the Topic:

In your own words, say to the students: *Our topic for today is, "We Worked Together to Get It Done." Many times we do things all by ourselves, but sometimes it is necessary or more fun to do things with other people. Think of a time when you did something with others. Perhaps you and a friend, or you and your family, worked together to finish something - like a Halloween costume, or a holiday dinner. Maybe you and your Mom did the dishes together, or you and a friend put together a puzzle. Have you and a brother or sister ever worked together to make cookies, or build a sand castle? Think about it for a minute or two, and when you are ready to share, please look at me. The topic is, "We Worked Together to Get It Done."*

Discussion questions:

— *Do you think it is easier to get the job done with other people helping?*
— *How did you decide who was going to do what?*
— *If you were going to do the same job again, would you do the part of the job that you did this time, or would you do a different part of the job? Which part?*

Your questions:

Someone Liked What I Did

Purpose:

To help students consider verbal and nonverbal cues in knowing what other people are feeling and to describe how their behavior can influence the feeling and actions of others.

Theme:

Relationship Skills

Introducing the Topic:

In your own words, say to the students: *Today our topic is, "Someone Liked What I Did." Think about something you did that one or more people liked. It could have been here at school or it could have been somewhere else. Maybe you did something that made one of your parents feel proud of you. Or maybe you shared something with a friend in your neighborhood. Perhaps you were polite to someone at church, or somewhere else, and the person really liked it. Think about it and look up at me when you are ready to speak and listen. Our topic is, "Someone Liked What I Did."*

Discussion questions:

— *We did things people liked. How could we tell they liked the things we did?*
— *Does it do us any good to do things other people like?*
— *How can you show a person that you like what he or she does?*
— *How can you tell if you do something someone doesn't like?*

Your questions:

How Someone Else's Decision Affected Me

Purpose:

To help students that decisions can have far reaching effects and to be able to examine the consequences of decisions.

Theme:

Relationship Skills

Introducing the Topic:

In your own words, say to the students: *We all make decisions every day. For instance, we decide what to wear and eat, how to act, what to do, and what to say. Many times, the decisions we make affect other people. At the same time, other people are making decisions too - and the decisions they make sometimes affect us. That is what we are going to talk about today. Our topic is, "How Someone Else's Decision Affected Me." Think of a decision that another person made that somehow affected you. Maybe someone in your family decided to bring ice cream home one night, and you were happy because you got to eat some of it. That decision had a good affect on you. On the other hand, maybe you have a friend whose family decided to move to another town and now you don't see your friend anymore. That decision had a bad affect on you. Perhaps a brother or sister decided to get a paper route, and now you spend a lot of time helping him or her fold papers. My decision to have a discussion group today was just a little one, but it affected you because you are a member of the discussion group! Think quietly for a moment or two, and look at me when you are ready. The topic is, "How Someone Else's Decision Affected Me."*

Discussion questions:

— *What were some of the decisions that other people made that affected us?*
— *How did they affect us?*
— *Why do the decisions we make so often affect other people?*
— *Has anyone ever asked you to help make a decision because you would probably be affected by it? How did you feel about that?*

Your questions:

How My Decision Affected Someone Else

Purpose:

To encourage students to understand that their actions affect other people and to help them get in touch with the idea of considering others in their decision making process.

Theme:

Relationship Skills

Introducing the Topic:

In your own words, say to the students: *Our topic for today is, "How My Decision Affected Someone Else." Have you ever made a decision and been aware that someone else was either helped or hurt by it? Maybe you made a new friend and decided to play with him or her practically every chance you got. How did your decision affect your new friend? How did it affect your old friends? Maybe you decided to go camping instead of to soccer or little league practice. How did that decision affect the other members of the team? Or maybe you decided to practice especially hard for a music or dance recital, or a karate demonstration. How did that decision affect your teacher? ...your parents? Other people are affected by the things we do, and also by the things we say. So being polite and telling the truth affect others— and so do being impolite and telling lies. Think about it for a few moments. Tell us about a decision you made, but concentrate on describing the affect your decision had on others. When you are ready to share, look at me. The topic is, "How My Decision Affected Someone Else."*

Discussion questions:

— *Why is it that so many of our decisions affect others?*
— *Can you think of any types of decisions that don't affect others?*
— *When should you think about the affects of a decision—before you make it or after you make it?*

Your questions:

A Time I Accepted and Included Someone

Purpose:

To help students develop understanding of how all persons need to belong and be accepted by others and to develop awareness of skills for getting along well with others.

Theme:

Relationship Skills

Introducing the Topic:

In your own words, say to the students: *People want to be treated in friendly ways by others. Everyone needs to feel liked, and most everyone wants to be invited to play or participate with others. Yet sometimes it's hard for us to accept a new person. So today, let's talk about times we were friendly to someone who needed our friendship— even if it felt uncomfortable. Our topic is, "A Time I Accepted and Included Someone." Can you remember a time like that? It could have been anywhere here at school, in your neighborhood, or at church. Perhaps someone new came along and you were nice to that person because you knew how he or she felt. Maybe you were the new person yourself once, and you remembered how much you wanted to be accepted and included at that time. Or maybe the person you accepted and included was someone you'd had a disagreement with, and he or she needed to know you* still liked him or her. *If you decide to share, tell us how you let the person know that you accepted and wanted to include him or her. Think about it for a few moments. When you are ready, look up at me and we'll start the session. The topic is, "A Time I Accepted and Included Someone."*

Discussion questions:

— *Does it mean a lot to people when we accept and include them?*
— *Why is it hard sometimes to show someone acceptance and to include him or her?*
— *Did anyone get any ideas for ways to treat someone when you want to accept and include him or her?*

Your questions:

A Promise That Was Hard to Keep

Purpose:

To help students observe themselves and to recognize their feelings and examine their actions. This topic also helps students to understand the consequences of their actions and to know if thoughts or feelings ruled their decision.

Theme:

Self Management and Self Awareness

Introducing the Topic:

In your own words, say to the students: *Today, our topic is, "A Promise That Was Hard To Keep." Notice that this is a topic that allows you to go either way. You can talk about how you kept your promise, or you can talk about a promise that proved too difficult to keep. When we make a promise, we are pledging our word. But sometimes we agree to something that, although it may not have seemed overwhelming at first, proves very difficult in the long run. Other times, we know right from the start that it will be tough, but for some reason we promise anyway. Think of a promise that you found hard to keep and tell us the circumstances, the outcome, and your feelings along the way. Please remember not to use names. The topic is, "A Promise That Was Hard to Keep."*

Discussion questions:

— *How do you feel about yourself when you are able to keep a promise?*
  ... not able to keep a promise?
— *How are promises related to honesty, integrity, and trust?*
— *What did you learn from this topic that you would like to mention?*

Your questions:

I Succeeded Because I Encouraged Myself

Purpose:

To help students understand the value of positive self-talk and that doubts are natural but can be overcome if we counteract them with encouraging words.

Theme:

Self Management

Introducing the Topic:

In your own words, say to the students: *Our topic for this session is, "I Succeeded Because I Encouraged Myself." Have you ever wanted to do something and weren't quite sure you could? Think of a time when you felt unsure, but encouraged yourself and, consequently, found a way to be successful. Perhaps you tried to teach your pet a trick, or needed to do a good job on a report for school. Maybe you were trying to master something on a computer, or were learning a new game. Whatever it was, you were not sure you could do it, but after giving yourself some encouraging words, you were successful. Take a few quiet moments to think it over. The topic is, "I Succeeded Because I Encouraged Myself."*

Discussion questions:

— *What do you think caused each of you to be successful?*
— *What kinds of doubts did you have to overcome to be successful?*
— *What do you think would have happened if you had used discouraging words instead of encouraging words?*

Your questions:

A Time I Taught Something to Someone Else

Purpose:

To stimulate in students the awareness that there are many possibilities for sharing knowledge and skills with other people and that sharing knowledge is an element of friendship building.

Theme:

Relationship Skills

Introducing the Topic:

In your own words, say to the students: *Today we're going to talk about a time when you knew something so well you were able to share it with someone else. The topic is "A Time I Taught Something to Someone Else." There are many situations in which people learn. Learning and teaching happen all over the place. Think about one time when you were the teacher and you showed someone how to do something or provided someone with information. This person could have been younger than you, or it may have been someone your same age. Or maybe it was an older person like a teacher. Whoever it was or whenever it was, tell us about it if you will. The topic is "A Time I Taught Something to Someone Else."*

Discussion questions:

— *Do you think there ever comes a day when a person can't learn anymore because everything has already been learned?*
— *What do you think of teachers being students sometimes and students being teachers?*
— *What do we gain by helping someone else learn something?*

Your questions:

My Reality Was Different from Someone Else's

Purpose:

To teach students that people can have different interpretations of the same situation. This topic also helps to develop foundation skills for understanding others and appreciation of differences as well as similarities.

Theme:

Relationship Skills

Introducing the Topic:

In your own words, say to the students: *Our topic today is "My Reality Was Different from Someone Else's." Native American's are famous for having their council meetings in a large circle. There are many important reasons for this. One of these reasons is that when something is placed in the middle of the circle, each person sees it a little differently. To the Native Americans this means that every person's perspective (view of reality) is different to some degree. Sometimes when we see or think about something in one way, we are surprised to find that someone else regards the same thing in a totally different way. Often we are both convinced that our reality is the correct one. This may affect our ability to make or keep friends, or make decisions. Think about it and see if you can find a time in your life when you've experienced this kind of situation. The topic is "My Reality Was Different from Someone Else's."*

Discussion questions:

— *What really is real, and who decides the answer?*
— *What can you learn about another person if you stop to consider their point of view?*

Your questions:

How I Got Someone to Pay Attention to Me

Purpose:

To increase students' awareness that receiving attention is a basic human need, and to focus on positive ways of getting attention.

Theme:

Relationship Skills

Introducing the Topic:

In your own words, say to the students: *The topic for this session is "How I Got Someone to Pay Attention to Me." When you or I want to communicate with someone, first of all we have to get them to notice us. We have to do something to get the other person to focus in on us. As you probably know, there are many ways to do this. You can do something funny, helpful, destructive, informative, exciting, or whatever, and people will automatically look at you. You are invited to share a time when you got someone's attention in some situation. Perhaps it was a challenging situation like trying to get the attention of a person in a large crowd who was a long way away from you. Perhaps you wanted to communicate a message to a group that you were leading. Or maybe it was a time when you got someone's* attention easily. The topic is "How I Got Someone to Pay Attention to Me."

Discussion questions:

— *Do people* really *need attention?*
— *Does the way you get attention have anything at all to do with the kind of attention you get or how long the attention lasts?*
— *What do you think a person who never received any attention would be like?*

Your questions:

Once When Somebody Wouldn't Listen to Me

Purpose:

To help students understand the importance of listening in getting along with others and in the communication process. It also points out the distinction between attentive, conscious listening and inattentive, unconscious hearing.

Theme:

Relationship Skills

Introducing the Topic:

In your own words, say to the students: *Today we're going to talk about some of the frustrations that occur in the communication process. The topic is "Once When Someone Wouldn't Listen to Me." Did you ever need to have someone listen to you, but they wouldn't? You've probably noticed your little brother or sister or even a pet, like your dog or cat, trying to get someone's attention. Maybe they were ignored or forgotten. Take a minute to think about it, and tell us, if you will, about a time when you had an experience like this. The topic is "Once When Someone Wouldn't Listen to Me."*

Discussion questions:

— *What similarities and differences did you notice in our feelings about not being listened to?*
— *What do you think are the best ways to handle the situation of not being listened to?*
— *Why is it important to listen to others?*
— *How do you feel when someone is really listening to you?*
— *What do you do when you know someone isn't listening to you?*

Your questions:

Something I Never Do When I Want to Keep a Friend

Purpose:

To help students describe how all persons need to belong and to be accepted by others and to demonstrate desirable skills for interacting with and relating to others

Theme:

Relationship Skills

Introducing the Topic:

In your own words, say to the students: *Today we are going to talk about friendship and what we do to keep friends. Our topic is, "Something I Never Do When I Want to Keep a Friend." No one is a perfect friend. But we can certainly avoid doing things that might cause us to lose our friends. Has anyone ever treated you in a way that made you decide you didn't want to be friends with him or her anymore? If so, you know better than to treat your own friends that way. Maybe someone broke a promise that he or she made to you. Or maybe you told a secret to someone and then found out that he or she repeated your secret to several other people. Perhaps you had a friend who never asked you over, or didn't invite you to her birthday party. Or maybe you lent a video to someone and he never returned it. It's good to know what actions to avoid if you want to keep a friend. Think of an example and tell us about it, but don't mention any names. Take a few moments to think about it. When you are ready, look at me. The topic is, "Something I Never Do When I Want to Keep a Friend."*

Discussion questions:

— *How do you feel when a friend treats you badly?*
— *How would our friends feel if we treated them badly?*
— *Does a real friend care how you feel?*
— *How do you let your friends know that you care how they feel?*

Your questions:

I Got Into a Conflict

Purpose:

To help students understand how one's behavior influences the feelings and actions of others and to describe healthful ways of coping with conflicts, stress, and emotions. It also helps students consider ways of dealing with reactions of others under stress and conflict

Theme:

Relationship Skills

Introducing the Topic:

In your own words, say to the students: *Our topic today is, "I Got Into a Conflict." Conflicts are very common. They occur because of big and little things that happen in our lives. And sometimes the littlest things that happen can lead to the biggest conflicts. This is your opportunity to talk about a time when you had an argument or fight with someone. Maybe you and a friend argued over something that one of you said that the other didn't like. Or maybe you argued with a brother or sister over what TV show to watch, or who should do a particular chore around the house. Have you ever had a fight because someone broke a promise or couldn't keep a secret? If you feel comfortable telling us what happened, we'd like to hear it. Describe what the other person did and said, and what you did and said. Tell us how you felt and how the other person seemed to feel. There's just one thing you shouldn't tell us and that's the name of the other person, OK? Take a few moments to think about it. When you are ready, look at me. The topic is, "I Got Into a Conflict."*

Discussion questions:

— *How did most of us feel when we were part of a conflict?*
— *What kinds of things led to the conflicts that we shared?*
— *How could some of our conflicts have been prevented?*
— *What could have been done by you to avoid the conflict?*
— *What did you learn from this topic that can help you manage future conflicts?*

Your questions:

A Time I Was Rejected for Something About Me That Was Different

Purpose:

To help develop empathy by allowing students to become more aware of how it feels to others, as well as themselves, to be rejected for something over which they have no control.

Theme:

Relationship Skills

Introducing the Topic:

In your own words, say to the students: *Our topic for today's session is "A Time I Was Rejected for Something About Me That Was Different." Our purposes for discussing this topic are to find out how things like this happen and to talk about how it feels to be unaccepted for something about you that you can't or won't change. So think of a time when this happened to you. If you decide to share, tell us what happened, without telling us who rejected you. Today's topic is "A Time I Was Rejected for Something About Me That Was Different."*

Discussion questions:

— *How are people affected when they are rejected for something about them that's different?*
— *Have we been talking about prejudice?*
— *What have you noticed or learned in this session that you would like to mention?*

Your questions:

It Was Hard, But I Said No

Purpose:

To allow the students the opportunity to identify thoughts and actions that can help control impulses when faced with difficult choices.

Theme:

Self Management

Introducing the Topic:

In your own words, say to the students: *Has anyone ever asked you to do something that you knew was wrong or not good for you? Maybe the thing this person asked you to do sounded like fun, so it was hard to say no—but you did. Things like that happen to all of us, not just while we're growing up, but even as adults so it's important to learn to say no. Today, let's talk about how we can do that. Our topic is, "It Was Hard, But I Said No." Think of a time when you really wanted to do something, but you knew you shouldn't, so you said no. Maybe a friend asked you to come over after school, but your mother wanted you to come straight home, so you said no. Or maybe someone asked you to trade your sandwich for a candy bar, but you knew that wouldn't be a good lunch, so you said no. Did anyone ever ask you to tell a lie so he or she wouldn't get into trouble? Or keep quiet about something? Or smoke a cigarette? Tell us about something like this that happened to you, but don't say who asked you to do it. Think about it for a moment or two, and look at me when you are ready to share. The topic is, "It Was Hard, But I Said No."*

Discussion questions:

— *How did you feel when you said no?*
— *What did the other person do or say when you said no?*
— *Why is it hard to say no?*
— *How can we learn to say no to people who ask us to do things that are wrong or bad for us?*

Your questions:

112

A Time I Made a Big Effort and Succeeded

Purpose:

To have students develop an awareness of feelings and behaviors that led to a successful experience and to appreciate the value of persistence in reaching a goal.

Theme:

Self Management

Introducing the Topic:

In your own words, say to the students: *Today we're going to talk about what it's like to accomplish something after trying very hard. Our topic is, "A Time I Made a Big Effort and Succeeded." Have you ever tried very hard to do something and finally succeeded ? Perhaps you worked hard to write a story, changing words around to make it sound better and adding descriptions and action verbs, and finally finishing a good copy that you were proud of. Maybe you practiced running everyday until you ran a mile without stopping. Or perhaps you planted a garden, watering and weeding it regularly. At last you were rewarded by beautiful flowers or delicious vegetables. Have you ever worked many hours to make a model or build something, like a fort? How did you feel about succeeding after having made such a big effort? Were you proud of yourself? Did you feel good ? Take a few moments to think about it before we begin. Our discussion topic is, "A Time I Made a Big Effort and Succeeded."*

Discussion questions:

— *How did we feel about succeeding after making a big effort?*
— *Why is it important to keep trying even when something is difficult?*
— *What is the difference between making a big effort and just wishing for something to happen?*
— *What did you learn about yourself from this topic?*

Your questions:

How My Mistake Helped Me Learn

Purpose:

To have students recognize that everyone make mistakes from time to time and to understand that mistake doesn't mean failure. This topic also helps students to view mistakes as learning experiences.

Theme:

Self Management

Introducing the Topic:

In your own words, say to the students: *When we make choices, we sometimes choose the wrong thing. We call this making a mistake. Our topic today is, "How My Mistake Helped Me Learn." We all make mistakes—and we all have a chance to learn some thing from every mistake we make. Mistakes are like good friends—they teach us things we need to know. Think of a mistake you made that taught you something. It can be a big mistake, or a small one. For example, maybe you tried to spell a new word and used the wrong letter, but making that mistake helped you learn to spell the word correctly. Or maybe you asked for a great big piece of cake with ice cream, and when your stomach hurt after wards, you learned not to take so much next time. Maybe when you were very young, you wandered off in the shopping center and lost your parents for awhile.*

How did you find them again, and what did you learn? Maybe you left your bike outside overnight and in the morning it was gone. What did that mistake teach you? Think quietly for a few minutes. Think of a mistake you made, and then think about what you learned from making it. Look at me when you're ready to share. The topic is, "How My Mistake Helped Me Learn."

Discussion questions:

— *Does everyone make mistakes?*
— *Is it OK to make mistakes?*
— *What can mistakes teach us about ourselves?*
— *If we let them, can mistakes be our friends? How?*

Your questions:

A Time I Handled My Feelings Well

Purpose:

To help students identify ways to express and deal with feelings and to demonstrate a positive attitude about self.

Theme:

Self Awareness and Self Management

Introducing the Topics:

In your own words, say to the students: *Sometimes we face situations that cause us to experience strong feelings. How we behave at those times depends on how well we take charge of our feelings. Today, we're going to talk about instances when the outcome was good. Our topic is, "A Time I Handled My Feelings Well." For example, maybe you wanted a special gift for your birthday or Christmas and didn't receive it because your parents either failed to realize how important it was to you or couldn't afford it. Since you didn't want to hurt their feelings, you didn't express your disappointment to them, but told a friend instead. Perhaps you were very angry at someone and wanted to hit the person, but instead managed to talk to him or her and express your angry feelings without hitting. Maybe you lost a game or an election and really wanted to yell, but instead congratulated the winner. Handling your feelings well usually means doing what is appropriate, without hurting someone else in the process. Think of a situation that you feel OK sharing, and when you are ready, the topic is, "A Time I Handled My Feelings Well."*

Discussion questions:

— *What similarities were there in the ways we handled our feelings?*
— *What differences were there?*
— *If our feelings are always acceptable, why isn't our behavior always acceptable?*
— *Which do we have to control, our feelings or our behavior?*
— *How can we do that?*

Your questions:

If your heart is in Social-Emotional
Learning, visit us online.

Come see us at
www.InnerchoicePublishing.com

Our web site gives you a look at all our other Social-Emotional
Learning-based books, free activities, articles, research, and
learning and teaching strategies. Every week you'll get a new
Sharing Circle topic and lesson.

INNERCHOICE Publishing
15079 Oak Chase Court
Wellington, FL 33414

CPSIA information can be obtained at www.ICGtesting.com
Printed in the USA
BVOW09s2242200316

441098BV00005B/81/P